Thomas Edward Kebbel

The Old and the New English Country Life

Thomas Edward Kebbel

The Old and the New English Country Life

ISBN/EAN: 9783337231187

Printed in Europe, USA, Canada, Australia, Japan

Cover: Foto ©Andreas Hilbeck / pixelio.de

More available books at **www.hansebooks.com**

THE OLD AND THE NEW
ENGLISH COUNTRY LIFE

THE COUNTRY CLERGY
THE COUNTRY GENTLEMEN
THE FARMERS
THE PEASANTRY
THE EIGHTEENTH CENTURY

BY

T. E. KEBBEL, M.A.

AUTHOR OF
'AGRICULTURAL LABOURERS,' 'ESSAYS IN HISTORY AND POLITICS,'
'LIFE OF LORD BEACONSFIELD,' ETC.

WILLIAM BLACKWOOD AND SONS
EDINBURGH AND LONDON
MDCCCXCI

PREFACE.

The public has recently shown so lively a curiosity touching everything connected with English rural life, that I should probably have been tempted to try my fortune with these sketches, even had no other reason existed for giving them to the world in their present form, and under my own name. But I have been prompted to do so by another motive as well. Some parts of this volume are only the reproduction in other words, of thoughts, opinions, and descriptions, first printed many

years ago, while others have been written
with more direct reference to passing events,
and the changed conditions of country society
which I have lived to witness. But the
interest which has been awakened in the
condition of the agricultural poor ever since
they were invested with political power has
brought, and is daily bringing, numerous
other writers into the field, in whose works
I often see embodied much that I was the
first to point out, both long ago, and only
yesterday. I am not so vain as to be ac-
cusing any one of plagiarism; but I hope I
may be excused for wishing to appropriate
to myself what is really my own, whether
it is true or false, good, bad, or indifferent.

The pictures here drawn of the older generation of clergy, farmers, country gentlemen,
and labourers, are founded on long personal
familiarity with all four; extending over a

period of more than thirty years, during which I lived among them, and had abundant opportunities of studying their habits, characters, and ideas. Since my home ceased to be in the country, I have continued frequently to reside there, and have kept up my knowledge of country affairs and country people down to the present time. This little book, therefore, whatever its faults or errors, is founded on actual experience; and on that kind of knowledge which comes from long habit, association, and sympathy, and is not hastily acquired to meet any particular demand. There are only one or two passages which form exceptions to the rule, and they are those which relate to the actual earnings and expenditure of the agricultural labourer, taken, with some other statistics, directly from my own work, 'The Agricultural Labourer,' of which a new edition was published in 1887.

These figures were, as I have stated in the text, derived from my own personal inquiries among the farmers and labourers themselves for the purpose of that particular work.

T. E. KEBBEL.

LONDON, *Oct.* 29, 1891.

THE OLD AND THE NEW.

THE COUNTRY CLERGY.

IN his notes to 'Waverley,' Sir Walter Scott remarks of certain changes which had taken place in Scotland between 1745 and the end of the eighteenth century, that they had made the Scotland of his own day as unlike what it was sixty years before as the England of sixty years before was to the England of Elizabeth. I have not sufficient knowledge of the country to say whether the further changes which have taken place since Sir Walter wrote have created as wide a gap between the Scotland of 1886 and of 1806 as existed between the Scotland of Sir Arthur Wardour and the Scotland of Baron Bradwardine. But of this I am sure, that

A

were any one to write a story of English rural life, entitled ' 'Tis Sixty Years since,' he would have to depict a state of manners almost as unfamiliar to the present generation as the manners drawn by Fielding and Richardson. George Eliot's earlier novels, 'Adam Bede,' 'Silas Marner,' and 'Scenes of Clerical Life,' have to some extent done this. But they belong to a still earlier period, the last ten years of the eighteenth and the first ten years of the nineteenth century, when not a ripple yet moved over the surface of rural society to tell of a coming change of weather. The influence of the French Revolution was visible in the large towns long before it penetrated to the secluded agricultural villages buried among their woods and lanes; and when rumours of it did reach them, the only effect was to intensify their natural conservatism and make them cling more closely than ever to the old order of things. But my own reminiscences refer rather to a time when the old and the new order of ideas were just beginning to meet each other; when it was yet doubtful whether railways would supersede or only supplement stage-coaches; and when the seniors, though they found themselves jostled here and there by strange theories of life and dress and government, did not suspect a revolution, and were rather irritated than alarmed.

The change in our rural society which has taken place since that time is nowhere so strongly marked as it is in the characters of the clergy and the better class of tenant-farmers. The squire has changed, but not so much. What he may become in a few years' time, it is hazardous to conjecture; but at the present moment the average English country gentleman of four or five thousand a-year is in all essential respects pretty nearly what he has been any time since the accession of Queen Victoria. Of the peasantry and smaller farmers the habits and ways of thought are still in a state of transition. The beginnings of a great change are undoubtedly perceptible, which in the course of another generation, when board schools and agrarian agitation shall have done their work, may complete that transformation in the character of the peasantry which has taken place in the classes just above them. But at present we see only the germs, and there are still nooks and corners to be found where we do not even see these. But in the clergy the change is very marked; and it is in the country villages that it is most conspicuous and most significant, and most closely connected with other great changes—moral, political, and theological.

The distinctive peculiarity of the country parson of the old *régime* was that he was part of a system. The village was a miniature of the State. The three estates of the realm were represented by the parson, the farmers, and the labourers, and over all was the squire. The little community was, under the old parochial system, self-contained and self-sufficing, with a life of its own, and with its own traditions and idiosyncrasy. What the Church was to the nation the parson was to the parish, and this embodiment of Church and State in every village in the kingdom represented with perfect fidelity for nearly a century and a half the preponderant public opinion of England. It expressed the Revolution compromise, according with the national repugnance to both Popery and Puritanism, which alone made the Revolution a success. On the barrier against both presented by the Established Church of England, the nation leaned as on a rock. The private lives of the clergy; the zeal or the indolence displayed by them in their special duties; the awakening or non-awakening character of their Sunday discourses,—were trifles not worth a moment's consideration alongside of the great truth to which the Church was a standing witness, and the safety of the great fortress of which she was a corner-stone. The shafts of Dissent, few and far between as they were, glanced harmlessly off the solid wall which the Church then presented to their attacks. In fact, the position in which the clergy lay intrenched was scarcely touched by them. Bolts aimed at doctrine or discipline flew wide of the mark, when doctrine and discipline had ceased to interest society, and when the Church's strength lay in her national character, and the double front which she presented against the two extremes of bigotry and cant, represented, however erroneously, to the popular intelligence by Popery and Dissent. It was an era in which her spiritual functions were, owing to the force of circumstances, subordinated to her political and social ones. Two hundred years of revolution, during which the nation had been tossed to and fro between the conflicting extremes of religious intolerance, had made it heartily weary of both. A decline of what is called spiritual activity, not of real sober-minded piety, was the inevitable consequence as soon as the combatants were exhausted. The nation sank back, as it were, into a kind of religious arm-chair, in which it slumbered peacefully till the beginning of the present century. The Church of England, therefore, not only represented the dominant political opinion of the Georgian era, but also the spirit of the age by which it was naturally accompanied — the comfortable easy way of taking things into which the English people settled down after the tumult of the Reformation and the Revolution had subsided. Wesley and Whitfield produced a great commotion; but the mere fact that the Church weathered it so easily, proves the truth of what we say — namely, that the foundations upon which she then rested were not touched by the declamations of the Methodists. Nor did they themselves wish to touch them. The Dissenters, for many generations, shared in the popular conviction that the existence of the Church of England as then constituted was, upon the whole, for the public good. As Englishmen they saw what their fellow-countrymen saw in the Church of England. They desired greater liberties for themselves, but years went by before they were hostile to the Establishment.

It is easy to see that the clergy who were brought up under this dispensation must have possessed a quiet undoubting confidence in themselves and their own position, which would give free play to all peculiarities, and relieve them almost entirely from any undue solicitude about public opinion. Such a position in every walk of life has its advantages and disadvantages. Virtual irresponsibility may lead to neglect of duty, to abuse of power, to selfishness and self-indulgence. On the other hand, freedom from restraint, and from the perpetual haunting fear of what the world will say, tends to make men more natural, more spontaneous, and therefore more likely to be listened to, than when they are less at their ease. In short, as a general rule, it makes the good better and the bad worse: and so it was in the Church of England. There were in those old days, it is but too true, many very bad clergymen, to whom what they called "parsoning" was a simple bore, and who excused, though they could not justify, the well-known saying of Sydney Smith. But of the large majority I believe that at least two-thirds were beneficial members of society, doing a great deal of good in their own way, and attaching the people to the Church by as strong ties as any which exist now. The other third were probably as active and zealous parish priests as any to be found even in these days of ecclesiastical revivals.

Of the country parson, who was indigenous to the kind of soil I have described, there were, of course, numerous varieties. Some, I think, are quite extinct. Some linger still in sequestered situations. But thirty or forty years ago there were many survivors of the old breed—men born in the last century, who were ordained and settled down in country livings while Lord Liverpool was Prime Minister, and who, though many of them had the sense to see that the revival of 1833 was historically unassailable, never took to it kindly, and seemed redolent to the last of high pews, black gowns, bassoons, fiddles, and parish clerks in top-boots. I myself, however, can recollect an older specimen than even these—one who, born before the death of Chatham, lived to see the death of Palmerston, and carried far down into the second half of the nineteenth century not only the habits and opinions, but even the costume, of the age of Pitt and Fox. He never had a pair of trousers in his life; and though it was to be gathered from his conversation that he had some time in his dandy days figured in boots and buckskins, my own impression is that when I knew him he had never worn a boot for forty years. In height he was about five feet eight; and was always dressed in a very broad-skirted black tail-coat, coming well up into the hollow of his head behind, a black single-breasted waistcoat, black knee-breeches, shoes, and gaiters. He wore no shirt-collar, but a voluminous white neckerchief wound round his neck in soft

thick folds, contrasting favourably with the tight
cravats and high "stick-ups" which were then in
vogue. On festive occasions he appeared, of course,
in black silks and silver buckles; and I can recollect
him when a young man of sixty-five or so wearing the
tight black-silk pantaloons which are chiefly known
to the present generation by the portrait of the late
Sir Robert Peel. He played a very good rubber,
and was a welcome guest at all the dinner-parties
in the neighbourhood, where he was treated with
great respect, and in his later years regarded with
much interest by those who met him for the first
time. He was fond of society, and well qualified to
shine in it, his natural gaiety and his old-fashioned
politeness mingling together very happily. But
much as he enjoyed himself abroad, it was in his
own home, in his own village, and among his own
people, that he sought and found the good of life.
He knew no pleasanter hours than those which he
spent in a round of cottage visits, chatting with the
mothers and grandmothers of the hamlet at their
afternoon tea, observing traits of character, local

idioms, and specimens of rustic humour, which it was his delight to retail in the evening to an appreciative circle at the parsonage.

The cottagers in turn were equally glad to see him, for, except in cases of illness, his conversation was of a secular character; and as he was skilled in horticulture, and learned, as Dominie Sampson would have said, in that which appertaineth unto swine and poultry, he was able to give them useful hints on these subjects, and sometimes left them wiser than he found them—a result not always, perhaps, attained by men of more spiritual zeal, who are fond of improving all occasions. Not but what, if either man or woman had been long absent from church, without being able to assign a good reason for it, he would administer a grave rebuke, all the more telling from his habitual easy good-nature. It was seldom that these visiting days did not result in one or more plates making their appearance at the parsonage dinner-table, to be filled with slices from the joint swimming in abundance of gravy, for some invalid parishioner whose case required good living. On a summer evening he delighted to stroll down his fields as far as the allotment-grounds which he had provided for the labourers out of his small glebe, and inspect their crops or their tillage; and I can see him now in the hay-field, with his hands in his pockets, and a benignant smile upon his countenance, as he exchanged jokes with the mowers or the rakers — there were no machines then — who might have had perhaps just a drop more beer than would have been altogether good for them at any other time than harvest, but who never forgot themselves, even under the influence of malt, in talking to the "parson," who, I don't suppose, ever heard a rude word uttered in his presence during the whole fifty-six years that he reigned over that little kingdom. He always dined with the village club at their annual feast, and watched with delight the rapid disappearance of the roast veal and batter puddings, which were considered the prime dainties on such occasions. He did not disapprove of a moderate hilarity, though he retired before the dancing began, only lingering long enough on one occasion to hear, to his lifelong amusement, a rustic gallant assure a young lady of his acquaintance that he " would kiss her if she wished it."

At home he found occupation in farming the few acres of land which he kept in his own hands, in pruning his apricot and apple trees, in keeping in order the shady walks which he had formed in various corners of his garden, in looking after the ducks, guinea-fowls, and turkeys which thronged his little farmyard, and in sometimes dragging the brook which ran through his meadows, and yielded good pike, eels, perch, and roach, which, as his sons grew up, were reserved for angling purposes. He was no sportsman, though very fond of natural history, and a student of the habits of birds, who built at their ease in the thick leafy covert which engirdled on every side his own snug ivy-covered house. He knew the eggs and the nests of every common bird that flew, and was always well pleased if his children brought him specimens of the rarer kinds, or of such as only haunted the more distant fields and brook-sides.

In this round of simple amusements our country parson passed his years, quite unaware that for six days of the week anything more could be required of him, or that the days were coming when zealots and bigots would

"Call his harmless life a crime,"

and the clergy would be summoned to exchange their sickles and their pruning-knives for the weapons of spiritual warfare, and their quiet game of whist and their pleasant village gossip for the "serious problems of humanity," which, in the language of the new school, are "everywhere calling for solution." That day indeed came even to this good old gentleman before he was called from his earthly home to a better one, where, let us hope, there are neither schools nor school boards, neither conscience clauses nor revised codes, and where payment for results having been made once for all, we shall, we trust, never hear of it again.

But our country parson always strove to do his duty according to his lights, and when the new order began to reveal itself, he made a manful effort to respond to the appeal. This was hard work at eighty years of age. He preached in his surplice, and had service on saints' days, and restored his church, and while his strength lasted did what he could. But neither he nor his people ever took kindly to the new ways. His sermons were of the good old style, inculcating the reality of Christianity, illustrating the doubts which might be thrown upon it after the fashion of Archbishop Whately, and insisting on the congregation believing in it as they believed in the history of England; which, by the by, did not go much backwarder with most of them than "Bony" and the battle of Waterloo. He was a beautiful and most impressive reader, thoroughly simple and unaffected, but combining great earnestness with those natural powers of elocution which no art can teach; and which lent a charm to the liturgy and the lessons, especially if taken from the Old Testament, such as once experienced could never again be forgotten. But when he tried to go beyond this he did not succeed. The people did not come to church on the saints' days. "The band" took offence at the harmonium; and after all, I think the bad chanting of a village choir was a poor exchange for the quiet pathos with which the white-haired patriarch in the twilight of a wintry afternoon used to repeat the *nunc me dimittas*. When the summons came he was in his ninety-sixth year, and though it was long since he had mingled in general society, it was felt in the neighbourhood that one of its landmarks had departed. "He was a great man among his people," said the greatest English Churchman of our own day, "and we shall have no more such in the Church of England of the future."

But "the country parson as he was" comprehends many other varieties, which have now however, for the most part, disappeared likewise. There was, of course, the hunting parson, as there is still, but who differed from the hunting parson of to-day as Adam before the fall differed from Adam after the fall. He hunted, and thought no ill: he knew not that it was wrong, or that anybody else knew it; whereas the parson who hunts nowadays does it in more or less of a defiant spirit, as a protest against "narrowness" —all denoting the more combative controversial stage into which we have now passed out of that peaceful Arcadia of mutual toleration. But I think the farming parson was a more decidedly special product of the old school than the sporting one; and that very few clergymen are to be found nowadays who farm in earnest on a large scale, and look to their profits for a substantial part of their income. There are in many parts of England, especially in the midland counties, livings with very large glebes attached to them, running from one hundred to six or seven hundred acres. The parson sometimes took the whole or a part of this into his own hands, and toiled as hard in his vocation as any born and bred agriculturist. He overlooked his men in the fields, and occasionally took off his coat and helped them, went to fairs and markets, bought and sold hard bargains, and was as good a judge of a beast as "e'er a farmer in the country." I can remember such a man well. He was a short, stout, plethoric man, with legs set on rather behind him, as some men's are, like a cochin-china's; and though active and robust, always rather waddled in his walk. One peculiarity which I think, however, he shared in common with all the men of that leaven, was that he always wore his clerical dress in whatever work he was engaged; and he might be seen on a winter afternoon, just as the teams got back from some outlying field, "serving" the pigs, or bringing fodder on a pitchfork to the cattle in the farmyard, in a full suit of black not very much the worse for wear. Nobody thought ill of such a man for his mode of life : it detracted in no way from the article of his spirituality. He went everywhere like other clergymen ; and his daughters, if he had any, would be refined and accomplished ladies. Odd as it may seem, there was nothing of the Trulliber about these men ; and what is perhaps still odder, is the fact that, in the case of the one whom I have more particularly in my eye, his sermons were abstruse and casuistical, devoted to such distinctions of interpretation and niceties of theology as one certainly would not have expected from his ordinary conversation and appearance. Perhaps the one was necessary to neutralise the effect of the other ; and the profound learning assumed in the pulpit on Sunday was intended to restore the balance, which had been sadly weighed down during the remainder of the week on the side of turnips, tups, and oilcake.

Then there were the clerical "bucks" and diners-out, whom I recollect still earlier in my boyhood. The comic curate, who came out to dinner in pale-green kerseymere tights—a man of family, an accomplished dancer, and asked to all the great houses in the county. Some of Miss Austen's clergymen, though not guilty of such audacities of costume, belonged, nevertheless, to the same type, and were doubtless considered excellent parish clergymen in their day. "How's your parson getting on?" said a country gentleman, who was somewhat of a humourist, to a very worthy cow-doctor who lived in a neighbouring village; "he's rather a queer sort, I understand." The parson in question was unhappily addicted to liquor, and what Johnson calls the lighter vices; but the man was in arms in a moment. "Queer, Sir Charles!" he exclaimed; "he's a most respectable man, barring his character!" Sir Charles told this story to his dying day with increased enjoyment of it every time. It was clear that in the man's eyes the parson was an institution. If his private character was bad, it was to be regretted; but it did not affect his position if his public duties were respectably performed.

Then there was the pleasant, middle-aged, free and easy, very gentlemanly parson, who was not perhaps much of a sportsman, though he might fish or shoot a little now and then, but was eminently the man of society, told the best and newest stories, joked with the young ladies, talked like a London clubman to their fathers and their brothers, affected the character of a thorough "man of the world," and dressed as little like a clergyman as he could. Before the rural conscience was awakened from its long sleep, such men were great favourites in society. They were often men of some little culture, fair scholars, and generally well informed. But they agreed with all the other varieties I have mentioned in the one common characteristic, that they did not consider their profession to entail on them of necessity anything in the shape of a distinctly non-secular character. They were part of the county society, belonging to a profession requiring the performance of duties more than ordinarily grave and serious, but when these were done not demanding of them any very different life from that of their neighbours. They were part of a great system, and that carried it off. Of course it is not meant that this conception was universal. Evangelicalism, in fact, was a standing protest against it. But Evangelicalism abode chiefly in the towns, and never laid any hold of the country people, whose minds are not the kind of soil in which emotional religion takes root. For all that Evangelicalism could have done in the majority of English villages, the country parson as he was might have gone on playing his rubber, farming his glebe, feeding his pigs, shooting his partridges, and taking an active part in country business to the day of judgment.

The old-fashioned parson and the old-fashioned peasant were thoroughly in harmony with each other. They looked upon Dissenters as Cobbett looked upon them. Church-goers saw no harm in attending "chapel" on Sunday evening, provided they had been to church in the morning; and the parson saw little harm in it either. The leading Dissenter in the village—a cantankerous man, too—used to say of the first old gentleman I have described that he was "a true Christian." A shoemaker in the same parish, of a figurative turn of mind, declared that there was "such a mess o' wickedness in the world that men wanted more than one hoss to pull them through it." Now and then the Dissenters, under the old *régime*, would be supposed to forget themselves, and carry their heads a little too high, as when they asked the parish clerk to tea—a liberty which he indignantly resented. But on the whole, the religious life of the village in those good old days Πρὶν ἐλθεῖν ὑίας Ἀχαίων glided smoothly along. The parson was accepted as part of the constitution —a country gentleman, a magistrate charged with civil as well as with religious functions, and sharing with the squire the duty of keeping order within a given district. As long as this conception lasted, so long was his position impregnable. The Nonconformist theory did not seriously affect it—indeed, scarcely touched it. The two did not meet upon the same ground. It was impossible that the work of the clergy as understood at that time could have been performed by any voluntary society. But in proportion as the clergy have lost their blended character, and come to rely more exclusively on their theological title to obedience, so far have they quitted their vantage-ground, and descended to an arena where Dissent can meet them upon something like equal terms. That they have gained much in exchange for what they have lost I should be the last to deny. But of that hereafter.

The old system wore itself out at last. Thanks to the vigour and patriotism of the English aristocracy, the revolutionary elements which existed in England, as they must exist in all old countries, did not catch fire from the French; and we escaped all violent disturbance. But we could not escape altogether. Privilege became unpopular. The Dissenters gathered strength and purpose. The repeal of the Test and Corporation Acts — and more, far more, the repeal of Roman Catholic disabilities; the Reform Bill, and the legislation which followed it; the new Poor Law and the Municipal Corporation Acts,—effected in the course of seven years a complete change in the position of the country parson, though its full effects were of course not recognised at once, and men of the old school went on as before, and the existing generation continued to think of them as before, long after the ancient *régime* had received its mortal wound. But this was not all.

There were men in the Church of England at that time who clearly understood what had happened between 1828 and 1833, and what was likely to follow, if something was not done. At that time, says Cardinal Newman, "I hated Liberalism." The triumph of Liberalism was to him like the triumph of Antichrist. And he and his friends set to work to arm the Church of England at all events for the coming struggle, and to find her a new, and, as they hoped, a stronger position instead of the one which she had lost, or was about to lose. It is no part of the design of this paper to discuss either the progress, the character, or the wisdom of the great Oxford revival. I believe it was, from a Churchman's point of view, a necessity of the period. But along with the vast amount of practical good which it undoubtedly accomplished, it certainly had this result also, that it damped the loyalty of the middle classes towards the Church of England. These were, and still are, rigidly Protestant. They had been shocked by Roman Catholic emancipation, and the proof of the Church of England's weakness which it seemed to afford. Still they would have allowed, perhaps, that so far the Church had done her best. She had fought the old battle over again to the best of her ability, and though her strength was not equal to the defence of the fortress intrusted to her, she had not betrayed it. But when Tractarianism made its appearance their horror knew no bounds. The Church, they thought, had voluntarily abdicated the position which alone gave her a right to their allegiance, and had gone over to the enemy. To understand the Anglican revival required, as Mr Cassilis said of Young England, "a doosid deal of history and all that sort of thing;" and of that sort of thing the middle classes were as innocent as Mr Cassilis himself.

The movement has had great success in reclaiming the masses of the working population, but it weakened the position of the country parson. The farmers and small tradesmen were almost to a man against it; and of course when the parson laid claim to higher spiritual prerogatives, his personal qualifications and his daily life and conversation were subjected to closer scrutiny. What the Tracts had done to loosen the relation between the parson and the farmer, the new Poor Law did to loosen the relation between the parson and the peasantry. Of this I feel more sure than of anything else which I have said in this chapter. I am old enough to remember as a child the way in which the labourers talked of the "Bastille." The substitution of a Union Board of Guardians for the ancient parochial organisation severed the old bond between the labourers and the landowners, whether lay or clerical, and, together with the new Ritual, has been one of the chief instruments of change in the position of the country clergy.

The country parson, as he is, presents as many varieties to the eye of the philosopher as his less active but more comfortable predecessor. There are among them, of course, "survivals," anachronisms, who, if they had lived sixty years ago, would have been more in their place. But these are few and far between. There are, as I have said, sporting parsons now as ever; but the parson who hunts nowadays, in the spirit of muscular Christianity — who hunts as Kingsley hunted, not only because he likes it, but to show that a clergyman has as good a right to hunt as any other man, and as a protest against asceticism, sacerdotalism, and modern exaltation of the hierarchic $\mathring{\eta}\theta o\varsigma$, in general — is wide asunder as the poles from the sporting parson of yore, innocent of all moral purpose, and hunting if he liked it, just as he got up or went to bed, without its even entering into his head that there could be two opinions on the subject. But the great point which the body of English country clergy of to-day seem to possess in common is, that they feel less strongly than they did that they are part of one great national system, and more strongly than they did that their position in the country depends exclusively on their personal efficiency. At first sight perhaps everybody might be inclined to cry out, And so much the better! But this I take leave to doubt. The proof of the pudding is in the eating, and if we take an average agricultural village of the present day, and compare it with what we can remember thirty years ago, shall we find that marked improvement in the manners and morals of the people which would be the best proof of the assertion? The moral influence of the Church of England, as a divine institution which was part also of the law of the land, and had the same claim on your obedience as the sovereign, the magistrate, and the Houses of Parliament, was quite equal, I think, to the effect which is produced by the increased individual activity of the parochial clergy. However this may be, that is certainly the distinction between the two epochs. The modern country parson is—not always, for there is not the same homogeneity about the class as formerly, but, generally speaking—always "on the go." He has penny readings, harvest-home festivals with a church service, lectures, entertainments without number. He strives most earnestly and laboriously to identify himself with the amusements of the people, as well as with their more serious concerns, and to show them that the Church is everywhere, and has as much sympathy with the joyous humanities of our nature as with its spiritual wants and troubles. All this is excellent. Only under the old *régime* it was taken for granted. Now the parson's life is one long effort. He is always to be seen in his long single-breasted coat and slouched billycock hat, hurrying at a half-run from one end of the village to the other, intent upon some new scheme for what is called "interesting the people." In a healthier state of things they did not stand in need of being interested. The *laissez-faire* principle is altogether banished from among the modern country clergy; and the difference between old and new is specially emphasised in their attitude towards Dissenters.

The country parson, as he was, looked on them simply as one of the minor troubles of life, of which, as no one could hope altogether to escape them, it behoved a sensible man to make the best. His way was to take no notice of them; to assume that they were all Churchmen, as by law they were, and to visit them and talk to them just exactly as he would have done to any other of his parishioners. This, I am afraid, the country parson of to-day finds to be almost impossible. The parson who was not only the clergyman but a good deal more besides, could do this; and in remote parts of England, where Dissenters who never enter the church door still seek the clergyman's advice in all temporal difficulties, he can do so still. But these are exceptional cases. The Dissenting minister now considers himself and the parson to represent two rival Churches, and the old relationship between them has been destroyed by the Dissenters themselves, even if the clergy had been anxious to preserve it. They now, however, seem to adopt one of two extremes in their dealings with Dissenters: either they live in constant suspicion and apprehension of them, tracking them from cottage to cottage, and labouring to counteract the poison which they have administered to each in succession—battling against them, preaching against them, thinking about them every hour of the day; or else they court them, try to make much of them, profess to believe that there are no essential differences between orthodoxy and heterodoxy, and go out of their way to pay them compliments and flatter them at every possible opportunity. If these clergymen suppose that Dissenters are really conciliated by this mode of treatment, they are very much deceived. If the difference between them were still, as it used to be, one only of doctrine and Church government, it might have that effect; but the difference now is social and political, and anything like "patronising" on the part of the clergy is silently, if not openly, resented. I hardly know which of the two above modes of dealing with Nonconformists is the more impolitic. The first is of course set down to incorrigible bigotry; the second to something very like fear. Yet so many things have occurred within even the last quarter of a century to alter the position of the Church of England both in town and country, that, as I have already said, the older relations between the clergy and Nonconformity are practically irrecoverable. These were based on a tacit recognition by Dissenters of the Church's national position, and acquiescence in her social superiority. But these are just the points which are now disputed; and it places the clergy, it must be owned, in a position of much greater difficulty than the one which they occupied when the present century was young.

I cannot too often repeat that these observations

consist of little more than "random recollections," and by no means profess to give an exhaustive account of either the old or the new school. They are general impressions, which I do not think however, will be pronounced substantially inaccurate by any one who has used his opportunities of observation. Human nature is human nature still; and in many respects the change in the country clergy is only in externals. Among the younger men, youth and its pleasures will still extort recognition; and though in our large towns there are many almost fresh from college who will deny themselves every amusement natural to their age that they may pursue with uninterrupted energy the work to which they have devoted themselves, there are others in the country where less self-sacrifice is demanded, who still, under different conditions, and allowing a much larger share of their time for parish duties, live very much the old life. Some, as we have seen, hunt and shoot: and the Tilneys and Eltons, the dancing and dining-out clergy of Miss Austen's novels, reappear in the lawn-tennis players and garden-party frequenters of the present day. Young ladies and young clergymen will find each other out as of old, if not in the ball-room, then in some other place which the world thinks proper for the time being to regard as more suitable for Churchmen.

Some clergymen of the new school take a delight, as some clergymen of the old school did, though from a wholly different motive, in dressing like laymen—always wearing black ties and coloured trousers, even in London. Some do this on grounds decidedly broad; others, perhaps for prudential reasons, from the fear of giving offence to sceptics by too ostentatious a display of "the cloth," which might possibly, they think, be construed as a menace; on the same principle, we suppose, which made the Duke of Wellington unfavourable to the display of military uniforms in the streets.

No sketch of the country parson as he was and as he is might perhaps be thought complete without reference to the rise and progress of ritualism. But it would be difficult to add much on this head to what I have already written without getting into deeper waters than would consort with the character of this chapter. I think that some part at least of what the Church has gained by ritualism in the towns she has lost in the counties; and that the farmer and peasantry preferred, and would prefer still, the parson of the old type. "It's not the likes of you, sir," said the village carrier to an elderly parson of his acquaintance, who was the best shot in the county, and sometimes made one at a pigeon-match—"it's not the likes of you as does any harm in the Church; it's them young pups," jerking his thumb as he spoke in the direction of a neighbouring church where a young curate had recently raised the banner of ritualism. I am afraid that in this elegant criticism there was a large element of truth; but I do not believe, at the same time, that the mischief is serious. The Church of England is just now in a transition state—always a period of some weakness and danger—but I see no reason to doubt that she will emerge from it with safety, and, it may be, stronger than ever. In calling attention to some of the salient characteristics of the era she is leaving behind her, and some of the peculiarities of the stage through which she is passing, I had no intention of judging between them, still less of presuming to say anything in serious condemnation of a movement which, if it has made the Church some enemies, has, I believe, made her still more friends, and which, at all events, had fifty years ago become almost unavoidable.

THE COUNTRY GENTLEMEN.

WHEN Sir Robert Peel told his party that he would rather be the leader of the country gentlemen of England than enjoy the confidence of princes, he was probably quite sincere. It was not merely because he was the leader of the Tory party that he was the leader of the country gentlemen of England. Mr Pitt had been the leader of the Tory party, yet it would hardly have been correct to describe Pitt as the leader of the English gentry. He was that and a great deal more. In the lifetime of Mr Pitt the position of the gentry was unchallenged. Their local and political authority, their administrative functions, their social relations with their tenantry and the peasantry on their estates, were untouched, and they stood in need of no championship beyond what was equally extended the whole constitution of the country. But after 1832, when our old territorial system received its first stab, the country gentlemen must have soon begun to feel that their own order was specially singled out for attack. The aristocracy, the great nobles with their thirty and forty thousand a-year, who moved in a wider orbit, and stood upon loftier eminences, and whose combined wealth and birth necessarily gave them an advantage over the claims of wealth alone—these for the present were secure. But the country gentlemen, the knightly order, whose importance depended on their local power, and the influence which they derived from the exercise of immemorial authority among their rural neighbours, were more immediately affected by the great democratic wave. The new Poor Law struck a blow at the old parochial system and those who administered it, which was not dictated solely by economic reasons, and it is now very commonly believed that the repeal of the Act of 1796 would have done all that was necessary at the time. The Poor Law was followed up by the agitation against the Corn Laws, avowedly conducted by its prime leader and instigator for the purpose of changing the aristocracies, and placing the mercantile in the place of the patrician order. The nobility were divided against themselves. But the country gentlemen found it necessary to draw together, and from that time dates what may be called the consolidated Toryism of the whole untitled aristocracy.

It was about this time that Sir Robert Peel made the memorable declaration to which we have referred; and if he had any sentiment in his composition, it may well have been evoked in favour of a class of men whose generous traditions and romantic history appeal so strongly to the imagination; which forms a link of such inestimable value in our social system; and of which he himself was, if a recent, at least a most distinguished, ornament. What might have happened had Sir Robert Peel and the country gentlemen never quarrelled, is a question which is often asked. Whether the prolongation of his life as the head of the Conservative party for another ten years would have permanently affected the course of events, and have appreciably diminished the force of that hostile blast which has been beating against his former friends ever since his death, it is impossible to say. All we have to remember now is, that the great nineteenth-century Minister, the man whom so many good Liberals believe to have been the greatest English Minister since Pitt, thought in such and such a manner of the country gentlemen of England; that he preferred their allegiance to the confidence of princes; and that to be their leader—not the leader of the Tory party, or the leader of the middle classes, but the leader of the English rural proprietors—was the proudest position he could occupy.

This is one testimony to the character of the English country gentleman. Another may be quoted from Sir Robert Peel's favourite pupil, Mr Gladstone. Speaking on the Irish Land Bill, on the 17th of February 1870, Mr Gladstone said:—

"In Ireland, from the unhappy circumstances of the country, . . . there has not rested in the hands of the landlords the discharge of that immense mass of public duties, bearing upon every subject of political, social, and moral interest, without fee or reward, which has honourably distinguished for so many generations the landlords of England. This fixed and happy usage I take to be a just relic and true descendant of the feudal system, which never took a real or genuine root in Ireland. . . . Are you prepared to denude them (the Irish landlords) of their interest in the land? and, what is more, are you prepared to absolve them from their duties with regard to the land? I, for one, confess that I am not; nor is that the sentiment of my colleagues. We think, on the contrary, that we ought to look forward with hope and expectation to bringing about a state of things in which the landlords of Ireland may assume, or may more generally assume, the position which is happily held, as a class, by landlords in this country: a position marked by residence, by personal familiarity, and by sympathy with the people among whom they live; by long traditional connection handed on from generation to generation, and marked by constant discharge of duty in every form that can be suggested—be it as to the administration of justice, be it as to the defence of the country, be it as to the supply of social, or spiritual, or moral, or educational wants, be it for any purpose whatever that is recognised as good or beneficial in a civilised society."

Since Sir Robert Peel was the leader of the country gentlemen of England, and since Mr Gladstone paid this well-deserved tribute to their services, many things have happened to impair their influence and their authority. But while they are still spared to us, let us take a glance at them as they now are, bating perhaps some slight change in their position brought about by agricultural depression; and consider very briefly how they stand affected by recent legislation, which it is thought by some will be their ruin.

There are, of course, several degrees of country gentlemen, as regards both fortune and family. I am using the present tense, because I am writing on the hypothesis that the losses they have endured from agricultural depression are not irreparable, and they may yet again be, if not all they once were, sufficiently like the present picture to make no alteration necessary. There are men with more than ten thousand a-year, and men with less than three. And between these two comes the largest class of all—those who can, or till lately could, afford to keep up large establishments in the country, with extensive gardens and pleasure-grounds, with six or seven hunters in their stables, and plenty of pheasants in their covers; but who do not regularly come to London for the season, or form a part of the fashionable world. They differ among themselves in point of birth, even more widely than in point of fortune. There is the squire or the baronet whose ancestor came in with the Conqueror, and there is the squire or the baronet whose grandfather was in trade, and who "bought out" some impoverished descendant of the Cavaliers. The *novi homines* are, as might be expected, numerous. But in England generally, the majority of the "county families" can boast of a respectable antiquity, reaching back, at all events, to Naseby and Edgehill, if not to Agincourt and Bannockburn. They are often, of course, the lineal descendants of the gentlemen who, under the Edwards and the Henrys, were the holders of knights' fees, and formed the flower of the feudal armies. As the tall barons were cut down by the Wars of the Roses, the knights whom they had overshadowed assumed a more prominent position, and became the founders of that order of country gentlemen which is often said to date from Queen Elizabeth. In process of time there came to be no distinction between the squires, or gentlemen who had not been knighted, and those who had; and after the institution of the order of baronets, knighthood lost its ancient military character and feudal meaning, and became gradually what it is at present.

Another source from which the order of country gentlemen was largely recruited lay in the numerous class of landowners who were not gentlemen of coat-armour at all, or even designated as squires. These were the "crestless yeomen" of Shakespeare; and it seems probable that between the accession of Henry VII. and the accession of Charles I., many of this class had acquired sufficient property and importance to become absorbed into the ranks of the gentry, and some of them, we fancy, held positions of high trust and authority among the English Cavaliers.

Of the estates of the Church confiscated at the Reformation, a considerable share, no doubt, passed into the hands of the gentry, and in some cases the property so acquired formed the basis on which new families were reared. By the dissolution of the monasteries, the lesser aristocracy, as well as the greater, was both extended and enriched.

The fourth tributary which has gone to feed the main stream is, as we have already mentioned, composed of successful traders, merchants, and professional men, who made fortunes and bought estates as they do now, and became after a generation or two as good country gentlemen as the Musgraves, the Knightleys, and the Bedingfields.

But whatever differences of birth or fortune may exist among themselves, the country gentlemen as a body agree in all essential particulars, receive the same education and breeding, possess the same tastes and habits, and to a certain extent exhibit much similarity of character. The boys go to Eton or some other of our leading public schools. In the holidays they learn to ride and shoot, and as soon as they can knock over eleven rabbits out of twelve, and jump their ponies over anything their own size, they are entered with the partridges, and make their appearance with the hounds. During their novitiate they make acquaintance with the farmers and their sons, who think it a great day when the young squire, at eleven or twelve years of age, first comes out coursing on his Shetland pony, which any one of them is proud to lift over the gaps, rider and all, though the little gentleman's dignity sometimes suffers in the process. In the summer evenings he plays cricket with the village club; and in these various ways becomes familiarly known to both the tenants and the labourers in the immediate vicinity of the Hall. He thus acquires an insight into the character of the whole class, and a knowledge of their wants, wishes, and prejudices, which can be obtained by no other kind of teaching. He comes to understand their language, and their peculiar modes of expressing themselves. He grows up in real sympathy with them; and in after-life his charities and his benignities lose all the eleemosynary or patronising element which is sometimes imputed to such favours, in the savour of personal affection and "auld lang syne" which still clings to them.

If the heir does not go abroad with his regiment, he probably travels a year or two after leaving college, and comes back to the old home to find his boyish friends sprung up into stalwart young farmers setting up in life for themselves, but still looking forward to settle where their fathers and forefathers have dwelt so long, at the first convenient opportunity. No sophistry can convince us that the relations so established between the owners and cultivators of the soil are not far more conducive to the public good than any which can possibly exist between capital and labour in our great cities. They prevent the irritation which is elsewhere excited by strong social contrasts unrelieved by the mellowing influences of hereditary connection and early personal intercourse; and they show the rich and the poor, the lord and the tenant, the superior and the inferior, living side by side, not only without any of the friction which the juxtaposition generates elsewhere, but in a condition of great social contentment, in which the

virtues of loyalty and respect on one side, and
liberality, confidence, and kindness on the other,
grow naturally and flourish, till the Radical demagogue appears, like the wild boar out of the woods,
to root them up. We say that the spectacle presented by a well-ordered English village, with a
resident squire and clergyman, such as was all but
universal thirty years ago, and is still rather the
rule than the exception, is the best rebuke to
agrarian agitation and Cockney ignorance that can
possibly be administered.

A glance at the country gentleman at home, and
his relations with his poorer neighbours, incline one
to believe, in spite of the odds which seem to be
against him in the approaching struggle for power
and authority in the counties, that the peasantry
may still be true to their traditions, and that even
where sentiment fails, self-interest may teach them
the wisdom of keeping the country gentlemen where
they are, and doing nothing to disgust them with
country life, or drive them away from their estates.

Take the Hall, or the House, or the Park in any
English county where agricultural depression has

not yet done its dismal work, and a walk through the gardens, the plantations, the stable-yard, and the out-buildings will show to what an extent it contributes to the employment of labour in the neighbourhood. The head-gardener must have his three or four assistants in the kitchen-garden, and as many more in the pleasure-grounds,—men who live in the adjoining village, and are employed all the year round at good wages. In the woods and plantings trees are being felled, underwood thinned, and fagots tied up. In the stables we find five or six hunters, besides hacks and carriage-horses, requiring the services of helpers, stable-boys, and blacksmiths, in addition to the regular grooms and coachman who live on the premises. Behind the stable-yard is the sawpit and the carpenter's shop, affording regular work to another group of the village population. The wives and daughters of these men will often be engaged by the housekeepers as laundry-women and needle-women. Take it all in all, will any practical man who knows what he is talking about pretend to say for one moment that the same amount of work, with the same degree of regularity, would be forthcoming for the peasantry and their families if the Hall were converted into a farmhouse, and the gardens and pleasure-grounds turned into grass or turnip fields? The notion is absurd.

We have taken the very lowest estimate of the number of men likely to be employed about the house of a country gentleman of moderate fortune. One who had a real, and not merely a nominal, income of nine or ten thousand a-year, would employ nearer double. But the stimulus to labour supplied by the House or the Hall does not end here. It extends to the neighbouring towns, where saddlers, cutlers, ironmongers, builders, brewers, and many other tradesmen would have to turn off half their hands if the country were emptied of all the squires and baronets who now occupy the manor-houses, and in well-known provincial phrase, "keep up the county." It is true, unfortunately, that "progress" has made great inroads upon the influence once exercised by the gentry in the class of towns above referred to. Before the days of railroads and stores the local aristocracy were among the best customers and patrons of the local tradesmen. On market-day the streets and inn-yards were full of carriages, bearing on their panels many an honoured crest and coat-of-arms. The shops were thronged with ladies whose household supplies were drawn exclusively from the linendrapers, grocers, and chandlers of their own county. The gentlemen, and very often the ladies too, lunched at the Bell, or the George, or the Swan: the smiling and prosperous landlord—there were no managers or companies then— standing in the porch to receive them with dutiful bow and frank civility, knowing them to be the mainstay of his fortunes. Those were the days of posting; and in the full tide of county gaieties, where distances were too great for a gentleman's own horses, the postboys were in regular demand, and another source of constant profit to the innkeepers. Now all this is changed. The ladies deal with the stores, and the gentlemen go in to their magisterial business by railway. Where twenty or forty pair of post-horses were kept sixty years ago, not more than two or three remain, and often not so many as that. The well-known equipages which had travelled the same road and stopped at the same houses for years, have vanished, and that tie, at all events, between the upper and middle classes, is now broken. If the Duke of Wellington really did say, when first he saw a train in motion, "There goes the English aristocracy," the sentiment, though exaggerated—as such *obiter dicta* generally are—did not altogether belie his proverbial sagacity.

If we think of the time when these words were uttered, we are carried back to a condition of society in which the government of the country by the landed interest still seemed to be in harmony with the constitution of things; and for a quarter of a century afterwards nooks and corners might be found, as perhaps they may be now, in which the feudal feeling still lingered, and the lord of the soil was an object of as deep reverence as Sir Everard Waverley or Sir Christopher Cheveril. One such we can remember ourselves. He was the head of a very ancient family originally settled in the north of England, and transplanted to one of the midland counties in the fourteenth century, where they had held the same estate in an unbroken line from father to son ever since. His property was in an exclusively agricultural and pastoral district, and must have been ten or twelve miles distant from any place that could be called a town. There was no other resident proprietor in the neighbourhood, and here he reigned supreme. He was a tall and very handsome man, with fine open features and curly auburn hair, the very model of a modern aristocrat as drawn by Mr Matthew Arnold, in whom, though light is not deficient, sweetness is the predominant characteristic. His dependants had all the benefit of this latter quality, and assuredly did not miss the former. The little grey village church lay close to the Hall, and the avenue by which Sir Richard and his beautiful wife and children walked down to it was visible from the porch. The parish clerk, when we knew him, had held that office more than a dozen years, but he still trembled at the great man's approach. "He's coming," he would inform the curate in an agitated whisper, as he discerned the stately figure of the baronet advancing slowly through the trees, and then hurry off to ring the congregation in—a ceremony always deferred till the appearance of Sir Richard gave the signal for it.

The tenants and labourers on this gentleman's estate would probably in those days have done anything he told them to do. But he never abused his power over them, was, though poor, an indulgent landlord, and, what perhaps was the great secret of all, lived and died among his people. All his pleasures, all his cares, all his ambition were centred in that one spot; and he never left it from one year's end to another. Such a man as this had no difficulties, and would have none now, about game-preserving or hunting, or any of the privileges or amusements of his order, which his tenantry were glad that he should enjoy, and did their utmost to promote. In the eighteenth century, and during the first quarter of the nineteenth, such as this man was, the bulk of the English gentry were. And such, in the opinion of some competent judges, they might again become would they only return to simpler habits, live entirely on their estates, and for weal or for woe throw in their lot with their dependants.

The only remark to be made on this view of the case is, that the gentry are doing so already under the force of circumstances; and hence, after all, may ensue the very curious result that the agricultural depression, which threatened at one time to estrange the tenantry from the landlords, may only end by bring them closer together.

"Though much is taken, much remains;"

and if the English gentry are not all they once were, they may, nevertheless, be strong enough to keep what they have got, and the very considerable share of power, respect, and popularity which still remains to them. We must all wish that it should be so, except those to whom the word "gentleman" is hateful. It is surely for the public interest that, scattered all over the country, should be little centres of culture, refinement, and the gentleness that comes of gentle birth; that there should be a class of proprietors in whose hands property assumes a less invidious aspect than it wears in large cities; and that the harsher intercourse of life should be softened, wherever it is possible, by the sympathies arising out of that "long traditional connection" which Mr Gladstone so cordially appreciates. We know that in our great towns it is impossible. What does a Londoner know of the work-people who minister to his various wants? of the glazier who mends his windows, of the blacksmith who shoes his horses, of the carpenter who makes his dog-kennel, of the bricklayer who repairs his garden-wall? Nothing—absolutely nothing. The country gentleman would know them all; would have a word or a joke for each, mingled with friendly inquiries after their wives and children, and an invitation to send to the Hall for something good if there were sickness in the household. The lady of the house and her daughters would all be frequent visitors at their cottages; the matrons of the village remembering the young ladies as little girls whom they have carried in their arms, and taking as much pride in them as if they were their own children.

Within a quarter of a mile of a house in Belgrave Square there may be families of labouring men huddled together in miserable lodgings of whom the rich man knows no more than if they were at Timbuctoo. But they know *him;* and look at him curiously across a wide gulf which is nowhere bridged over by the kindly charities and courtesies of country life. If this gulf is rightly considered one of the most threatening features of our present social state, surely that system is entitled to some degree of credit which helps to confine it within certain limits, and to keep one great division of English society free from its injurious effects.

We are sometimes told that the agricultural poor have outgrown their old relations with the clergy and gentry, and instead of being gratified with their attentions resent them as savouring of condescension. The village grumbler is no stranger to myself. There will always be somebody in such places who conceives himself to have been wronged in the matter of coals, blankets, or soup, and consequently views the whole system with a jaundiced eye. I am perfectly familiar with this species of discontent and the language in which it finds expression. But I am also certain, from long and wide experience, that it no more represents the real mind of the agricultural labourer, than the snarl of a disappointed politician represents the general sense of those with whom he generally acts. Both are supposed, by persons ignorant of their value, to mean a great deal more than they do: the mutiny of a whole party or the disaffection of a whole parish. They mean nothing of the kind. In some of our villages, no doubt, ideas have been put into the labourer's head, and words into his mouth which are not really his own, but which he thinks at first sight very fine, and reproduces whenever he has a chance. And it is also quite true that the kindest and best disposed of landlords or clergymen may be deficient in that special graciousness which clothes a benefit conferred in the garb rather of sympathy than of charity. But whatever sounds of discontent may proceed from either of these two sources, are like the chirp of the grasshoppers described by Burke, compared with the silent satisfaction of the other inhabitants of the meadow. Defects of manner are not confined to any one class of benefactors, and would probably be found more prevalent in urban than in rural districts.

If we follow the English gentleman from his home to the bench of magistrates, we shall find him in the discharge of functions for which his intimate knowledge of the habits and customs of the people peculiarly qualify him, which he and his forefathers have fulfilled for centuries with recognised efficiency and integrity, and with a stricter regard for the pecuniary interests of their neighbours than any public board is likely to exhibit. "The county magistrates," said the present Lord Derby, a man not given to the indiscriminate effusion of sentimental eulogies, "have never been guilty of a job;" and undoubtedly if the counties, like the nation at large, desire to be governed cheaply, they are not going the best way to work for the attainment of that object by cashiering their present public servants.

As the criminal business at quarter sessions is still to be left with the magistrates, the rural public will not be deprived so far of the benefit of their local experience—a kind of knowledge which is far more necessary in dealing with the class of cases usually brought before the magistrates than it is in the superior courts. One great advantage of the present system is, that country gentlemen are not obliged to depend so exclusively on the police for the information they require about the prisoners as those magistrates necessarily are who do not possess the same knowledge of the rural population. When a prisoner is brought up before the bench, the squire or the parson can tell at a glance to what section of the country people he belongs, and calculate the antecedent probabilities of his guilt or innocence with considerable accuracy. They will understand the full significance of many apparent trifles which would escape less experienced observers, and the triviality of many incidents which to others might appear to be important. More than this, they can tell better than anybody else could whether the offence committed by any particular prisoner is a specially bad one of its class, and bespeaks criminal propensities in the perpetrator, or whether the extenuating circumstances which may be alleged in mitigation of it are really deserving of consideration. No criminal judge, a stranger to the people, could tell this so easily as a country gentleman; and the importance of being able to do so is in proportion to the petty character of the offences which are commonly brought before the bench.

Of the purely civil duties, till recently discharged by the country gentlemen, some still remain to them, and some are still exercised by them in conjunction with popular representatives. The county magistrates are *ex officio* Guardians of the Poor, and being so, are also members of the "Rural Sanitary Authority" in each Union, and of the Highway Board in each highway district. They assessed and levied the county rate; they were intrusted with the execution of various Acts of Parliament; they granted liquor licences; they were and are visitors of prisons and lunatic asylums; and, in short, used to superintend and set in motion, either in whole or in part, the entire administrative machinery established in the English counties—that "immense mass of public business," as Mr Gladstone calls it, "without fee or reward," and in a manner which has "honourably distinguished them for many generations." It ought, one would think, to have been some very grave and pressing necessity that dictated even the partial abolition of such a system as this. The analogy which it is sometimes attempted to set up between county councils and town councils is entirely fallacious. Town councils, to begin with, sprang out of the necessity of filling up a vacant space. The abolition of the old corporations was not due to any uncontrollable thirst for representative government on the part of the Ministry of the day. They were described — rightly or wrongly is nothing to the purpose — they were described as hotbeds of jobbery and corruption, such as public opinion could no longer tolerate, and *therefore* they were condemned to death. These being abolished, it was necessary to put something in their place, and a representative council was most in accordance with the prevailing sentiment of the period. But had the old corporations been then what quarter sessions are allowed to be now, even by Radicals themselves, they might have existed down to the present moment. In fact, the history of the Municipal Reform Bill is only a repetition of the history of the Parliamentary Reform Bill which preceded it. This, too, was primarily intended to put an end to what was thought a bad system, and only secondarily to establish a new one. It was a disfranchising Bill first and an enfranchising Bill afterwards; and when Lord Lyndhurst carried an amendment reversing this order of ideas, the Ministry held it fatal to the Bill, and resigned at once.

In the second place, county councils have been called into being under very different circumstances from those which attended the birth of town councils, and invested with powers capable of being used for purposes of a very different character. To the agrarian agitation which has been carried on for many years in the English counties there was never any counterpart in the towns. Class has not been set against class in Birmingham and Ipswich as they have been in Warwickshire and Suffolk—and for this reason indeed, if for no other, that the particular kind of differences which exist in the rural districts do not exist in the towns. In the latter, there has been no doubt a sharp struggle between capital and labour. But the squire has

not been assailed only, or chiefly, as a capitalist.
He has been represented as a survival of feudalism,
a social tyrant, a privileged and exclusive aristocrat,
a cock whose comb must be cut without further
delay if the people were ever to hold their heads
up. Class jealousies, we repeat, are at work in
the counties on a much larger scale than in the
towns; and we must remember that, in virtue of
the very functions which the new councils are to
exercise, they will be armed with the necessary
weapons for gratifying these class jealousies.

But for all that it may still be in the power of
the gentry, if they choose to exert themselves, so to
demonstrate their superior fitness for the work of
local government and their readiness to administer
it with due regard to the rights of all classes, as
not only to cut the ground from under the agrarian
demagogue, but to check the progress of democracy,
and even make their own position stronger than it
was before. We may fairly suppose that some part
of the confidence with which the Government in-
troduced this measure was due to their reliance
on the good sense, patriotism, and magnanimity of

the country gentlemen, and the assurance that if, under the new system, they took the lead in county business to which they are entitled, their proved talents for business would enable them to keep it. There is a bright side to the picture as well as a dark one. We have met with English county members who say that here is a great opportunity for the country gentlemen; that they have now the chance offered them of showing what stuff they are made of, and of taking the lead in their respective counties more decidedly than they have ever done before.

We are very far from saying that there is nothing whatever to justify these more hopeful anticipations. On the contrary, we should be surprised to find that long habits of hereditary respect and well-deserved affection had disappeared in a day. The strength and tenacity of these very sympathies are part of our present thesis. But at the same time we must not allow ourselves to forget that the gentry will now have quite a new class of adversaries and a new kind of influence to contend against. The Radical candidates for the county and district councils will not be the same class of men as the Radical candidates for the House of Commons. They will be well-known local busybodies who, while not aspiring to Parliament, know quite enough of local affairs to be able to impose upon the ratepayers: to persuade them that county government has hitherto been an Augean stable which it is their special province to cleanse; and that they are the heroes for whom is reserved the honour of slaying all the local tyrants represented by "squires and spires."

It is true, of course, that the one concession for the sake of which alone the gentry and farmers have ever demanded county boards, was entirely dependent on the creation of some new authority in the counties, with a large infusion of the representative element in its composition: we mean, of course, the contributions in aid of local taxation. This seems very often to be forgotten. It is true that what is an act of justice ought not to be made the subject of a bargain. But we must look at facts as they are; and it is certain that the desired relief could have been granted on no other terms. This was not the fault of Lord Salisbury or the Conservative Government, but of the Liberal party in the House of Commons, and of the state of public opinion in general.

At all events, before we quit the subject, we would once more impress upon the country gentlemen the duty of making a great effort to overrule this measure for good. A concession to the spirit of revolution it undoubtedly is, of which the real character and tendency are not to be explained away by the fact that past mistakes have made it necessary. But anything less would have ended in something worse; and, starting from this conviction, the country gentlemen, if they deserve what has been said of them by their panegyrists, will strain every nerve, in justice to themselves, their ancestors, and their posterity, to bring good out of evil, and so to associate themselves with the new county administration as to make it the means of allaying agitation in the rural districts instead of provoking or inflaming it. Mr Chaplin, speaking in the House of Commons,[1] expressed a doubt

[1] April 1888.

whether the country gentlemen would care to contend for the mastery with the new forces arrayed against them. Our answer is, *noblesse oblige*. They are bound by a thousand traditions, and by every dictate of honour and patriotism, not to shrink from such a conflict, however mean and vulgar its accessories. They have to save the country they have helped to make, and to save democracy from itself. The end should dignify the means. It has been the evil destiny of all democracies to drive the best men out of political life. But to many of the general rules which historians and philosophers have deduced from their observation of popular government in the world at large, England has shown herself an exception. Let it be the ambition of her country gentlemen to keep her in the same path, and add another exception to the number.

> "Hac ego sum tantis dignus majoribus, auctam
> Hac trado natis nobilitate domum."

The path of duty lies through worse things sometimes than thorns and flints—through dreary wastes or noisome swamps, and among creeping things innumerable. But it may be the path of glory for all that.

We hope in this case, however, that the anticipation may be worse than the reality. The country gentlemen have large claims on the confidence of the peasantry. They have been foremost in all good works undertaken for their benefit—in allotments, in co-operative farms, in improved cottages, in school charities, and recreations. They have had little or nothing to do with the wages question. And the labourers, it is needless to say, know quite enough of the subject to be well aware that in ninety-nine cases out of every hundred the squire has pared his rent-roll to the quick. What with reduced rents here, and farms unlet there, they know that it is out of his power to make any further reductions, such as would enable the farmers to pay higher wages, without shutting up his house altogether,—a result for which another sixpence a-week would be no adequate compensation.

When "landlordism" is talked about in England, do those who abuse it know anything of the real truth? Do they know of the social privations and even hardships which, all over England, have accompanied the reduction of rent and the remission of arrears? They have still, it seems, to learn how largely the peaceable and uncomplaining attitude of the English farmers under their almost unparalleled misfortunes is due to the present consideration and sympathy of their landlords, and the influence of old associations handed down from generation to generation. Those who, in an age of revolution and lawlessness, contribute so largely to the maintenance of a better class of feelings among the people, may be rightly styled public benefactors. But they hardly deserve the name who, either from a desire to curry favour with the mob, as the shortest road to political success, or, what is even worse, from social jealousy, vilify, deride, and calumniate the English country gentleman from year's end to year's end, though he is all the time engaged in fulfilling some of the highest duties of a citizen, and in preserving those moral relations between the higher and the lower orders without which no society can long prosper, and which really lie at the foundation of all national happiness?

We may be thought, perhaps, to be verging on more debatable ground when we approach the subject of field-sports. Yet we challenge contradiction when we say that had a plebiscite been taken in the English counties a dozen years ago, hunting and shooting would have been supported by overwhelming majorities. The noisy few who complained in the newspapers or at public meetings, were a very small minority indeed; and nineteen-twentieths of the farmers would have readily allowed that they owed a debt of gratitude to the country gentlemen for keeping up the hunt, rather than any grudge for riding over their fields or preserving too many foxes. At the meet of the hounds they chat together, not of rents and prices, but of their respective mounts, the last good run they had, and the chances of finding the fox which, according to the gamekeeper, lies in the neighbouring osier-bed. Before they are off, perhaps a parson trots up, one of the old school, a doctor from the nearest small town, a lawyer, and a banker who is in a position to wear a red coat, and likes to meet his customers in the hunting-field. Hanging on the skirts of the hunt are a body of foot-people—the tailor, the cobbler, the stockinger—from the adjoining village; men prepared to run with the hounds all day, and enjoying the sport as much as my Lord or Sir Richard. Now, if it were not for the country gentlemen all this would be impossible. They it is who, far more than the nobility, support the hounds, look after the covers, and protect the foxes. They it is who bring all classes together, rich and poor, in the pursuit of a common amusement, in which all distinctions of rank are forgotten, and the best and boldest rider is the most honoured. Hear the foot-people, as they walk home, or take their beer at the public-house in the evening, discussing the run, and you will soon know whether the English villagers are hostile to fox-hunting or not.

The peasantry themselves nourish no antipathy to shooting. They are not very logical; they have no objection to a system which gives them two or three couples of rabbits in the winter, and congenial employment as beaters when the woods are shot. But they grumble at being punished for poaching, though, unless the game were preserved, there would be nothing either for themselves to poach or for the gentry to shoot. I think they would decidedly be opposed to any legislation of which they saw clearly that it would put an end to shooting, with all its incidental "extras." No gentleman makes himself unpopular by keeping up his shooting for himself and his friends, provided he can wink at an occasional delinquent, and takes good care not to have a bully in his gamekeeper. With the farmers the case is somewhat different. Now that the Ground Game Act has been passed, and they can kill the hares and rabbits as they please, they have no grievance against the game laws. What the farmers want is not to get rid of the game, but to get possession of the shooting. But these, again, are a very small percentage of the whole number; and the feeling itself is one of such very recent date, and so utterly irrational at the same time, that if it were not made use of by politicians for ulterior purposes, it would soon die out. Farmers should remember, whenever the question of property comes to be at issue between themselves and their landlords, that possession is nine points of the law; and that if either of the two parties is compelled to give way to the other, it will not be the proprietors, as long as they can still fall back on the alternative of cultivating their land themselves, and putting an end at once to all squabbles about tenant rights, rent, or sport.

It may be noted here, that at the reform of the game laws in 1831, no prejudice at all existed against game-preserving in the minds of the Liberal party. Their object was to enable the gentry to sell their game, so that they might drive the poacher out of the market.

We have spoken of the value of the country gentlemen as provincial administrators and magistrates, and as exhibiting before the eyes of the people the principle of property in a more amiable and attractive form than it presents elsewhere. We have yet to say a few words on the element which they contribute to the national character as a whole, in which we do not know that their highest value, after all, is not really to be found. There have been good and bad, wise and foolish, country gentlemen, as there have been good and bad, wise and foolish merchants, lawyers, and doctors ever since the order existed. And in former times, when travelling was difficult and even dangerous, when books were scarce and education what the pupil chose to make it, and when there was nothing to take a country gentleman to London unless he was a member of Parliament, it was only natural that his habits and his language should occasionally correspond more nearly than they have done since with those of the classes just below him. Macaulay's country gentleman, like Macaulay's country clergyman, is of course a gross caricature; but still of necessity with some elements of truth in it. The more good-natured Addison, who drew his Roger de Coverley, also drew the Tory fox-hunter. But in the present day, when we can rush from London to Cairo in the time which it formerly occupied to ride from London to Newcastle; when the best literature of the day is to be found on a country gentleman's table, and he is no stranger either to the beauties of art or the discoveries of science; when he has travelled, seen the world, and mingled in the best society,—the country gentleman of £5000 a-year is intellectually as different from his ancestor in the reign of George 1. as that ancestor was from Oxford, Halifax, or Queensberry. With these mental and social accomplishments, however, he retains the love of country life and the more simple and masculine habits which belonged to his forefathers: and it is this combination of hardihood and refinement, this happy admixture of sylvan tastes with urban culture, that imparts its distinctive and differential feature to the character of the present race of country gentlemen. The titled aristocracy of course possess the same qualities, and exercise the same kind of influence on the national character. But they are too few in number to exercise it with the same effect and on the same scale as the gentry who are always resident in the same place, and who know every man, woman, or child upon the land.

This character is something to be preserved and cherished. As an ingredient for leavening the national character as a whole, it is simply invaluable; and the extinction of it would be nothing short of a national calamity. That so deplorable a result is likely to be accelerated by the legislation to which we have here briefly called attention— by that "disestablishment of the squirearchy," as Mr Caine calls it, and of which the Radicals are now boasting with a light heart — I, for one, do not believe. It would be contrary, indeed, to all experience if the provincial aristocracy—excluded from the public duties which it was once their privilege to fulfil, and deprived of that authority over the people which the discharge of them naturally confers, living only for themselves, and caring less and less for the hereditary domains which would have thus been robbed of half their value —were able long to maintain either their social or territorial position. There is good reason to hope, however, that the country gentry may yet survive to disappoint those ingenious schemers who, under cover of reforming an administrative system, are bent on overthrowing a social one, and behind their affected enthusiasm for a principle, are concealing their jealousy of a class. I feel sure that the catastrophe may be averted, if the gentry take that view of their obligations which we can hardly doubt that they will take. "We have all lived long enough when we die with honour," says the old cavalier; and if further resistance to the forces of anarchy shall ultimately prove in vain, let it not be said of English gentlemen that they resigned the field to their enemies in any fit of petulance or despondency, or till every effort had been made, for the sake of the entire nation, to preserve that ancient social fabric which has been to the people of this country "the giver of ten thousand blessings."

It strikes one as remarkable at first sight that when the House of Commons consisted much more largely than it does at present of country gentlemen and their connections, the great majority of whom would be addicted to field-sports, the time abstracted by their parliamentary duties from the hunting and shooting season was larger than it is now. Yet such was the case. Down to the close of the last century, in the ordinary course of business, and when there was nothing particular demanding the attention of the Legislature, the meeting of Parliament was generally fixed for November or the latter end of October. The prorogation then usually took place in May or June, or else early in July. And the English love of rural life was gratified by the commencement of the holidays before the conclusion of the hay-harvest. Thus we find, on dipping at random into the parliamentary history, that the session of 1747-48 began on the 10th of November, and ended on the 13th of May; the session of 1748-49 began November 29, and ended May 11; the session of 1749-50 began November 16, and ended April 12; the session of 1750 on January 17, and ended June 25; the session of 1751-52 on 14th November, and ended March 26; the session of 1753, January 11, and ended April 17; the session of 1772-73 on November 26, and ended July 1; the session of 1773-74 on November 30, and ended May 26; the session of 1774-75 on October 26, and ended May 23; and the session of 1776-77 on October 31, and ended June 6; and so on to the end of the first five-and-twenty years of George III.'s reign. Down to that time the session which began after Christmas or ended after midsummer was a rare exception. With the accession of Mr Pitt to power, a slight change becomes apparent, but it was very gradual. And even after the French Revolution, though it ceased to be the rule to call Parliament together in November, it was frequently done, and it was not till about seventy years ago that the practice began to be looked upon as exceptional, and to be resorted to only in emergencies. What caused the change we have not been able to discover. Why it was that with the commencement of the present century the practice set in of deferring the meeting of Parliament to the beginning of February, no veteran senator still survives to tell us. But we may hazard some speculations on the subject, and the partial solution they suggest may be thought, perhaps, not devoid of plausibility.

At the beginning of the present century the habits of the English aristocracy were in a transition state. We know that before that great convulsion which placed a sword between France and all the rest of Europe, there was a numerous section of the English nobility and gentry who made the French *noblesse* their models, and were as miserable when they were away from Paris as if they had been Frenchmen born. These men helped to keep up that distinction between town and country gentlemen with which we are all so familiar in the comedy of the eighteenth century; between those members of the territorial aristocracy who filled the theatres and coffee-houses of London, and were the heroes of the fashionable world, and those who lived on their estates, and were content to be known as country squires. It mattered nothing to men of the former stamp when Parliament met or when it was prorogued. They spent their lives between London and Paris, and though they were always only a small minority, still they set the fashion, and there were not enough fox-hunters in the House of Commons to exercise any material influence on the arrangement of the session. Shooting rather than hunting seems to have been the favourite amusement of the upper classes; and it was not till the French Revolution, by stopping our intercourse with the Continent, threw the English aristocracy more exclusively on their own resources, that fox-hunting assumed its present proportions, and the distinction between a fine gentleman and a fox-hunter gradually ceased to exist. Concurrently with this change we find the meeting of Parliament growing later and later; and though we do not mean that the one change was the direct parent of the other, we should not be surprised if, indirectly, it had a good deal to do with it. It is true that princely hunting establishments had long been kept up at Goodwood, Woburn, Althorpe, Belvoir, Badminton, and Berkeley Castle. The Belvoir Hunt can boast a pedigree of nearly a century and a half, as it was regularly established in the year 1750. The Badminton Hunt dates from 1762. But for all that, the regular London man of the days of Horace Walpole, could he wake up at the present day, would stare his eyes out were the most accomplished performer in a London ball-room, the wittiest talker in a London club, and the best dressed man in the Park or St James's Street, pointed out to him as the best man across country from Melton to Harborough, or one who could ride in the van of the Pytchley from Naseby to Kilworth. Before

F

this fusion took place it is easy to understand why Parliament should have met in mid-autumn and been prorogued in May. The ladies naturally preferred London in the winter. The men shot their pheasants in October. Hunting, too, began earlier, and there was usually a good recess at Christmas. Even after the change, however, it was found difficult for a long time to combine the two pursuits—that is, of politics and sport; and it was during this interval that we read of such men as Lord Althorpe and Assheton Smith hurrying up to town after the day's run to vote on some important question, and rushing back again next morning in time to meet the hounds.

But if the exigencies of sport extended the season to February, the sportsmen had all the advantage of it. That is to say, no one for more than half a century dreamed of turning it to political uses. It was what it professed to be—the Parliamentary holiday: and as Governments in those days remained in power for long terms of years, supported by combinations which, compared with modern ones, were founded on a rock, there was really nothing to be gained by prolonging the parliamentary warfare into the autumn months. This is a very important factor in the result we are considering. It was not worth while in those days for the country gentlemen to sacrifice their ease, their pleasures, and their home duties to a series of autumnal campaigns either for or against the Government of the country. Now it is.

The enormous constituencies created by the Act of 1885 have not, indeed, created what is now commonly called "Parliament out of session," but have invested it with quite a new character. Every constituency is now an open field, and there is hardly a single one of which it can be predicted with absolute certainty that it will return either a Conservative or a Liberal. All are open to attack. There is no such thing as a safe seat or a close seat left, unless it is at our principal universities. The consequence is, that the process of attack and defence is always and everywhere going on almost from the termination of one general election to the beginning of another. This cause alone has multiplied the number of public meetings in every constituency by ten or a dozen fold. Some emissary from the enemy's camp is always in the field; the sitting member is always on his defence; while at the same time each individual of the party is obliged to contribute his share towards the general defence or general indictment of the Government, which is being conducted on a larger scale by his leaders. Of the whole House of Commons, therefore, only a very few lucky members find the recess a period of repose. In the old days no county or borough member was expected to address his constituents more than once a-year. A quiet little meeting in the county town, a haunch of venison or a few brace of pheasants, and a speech of half an hour's duration, were all that was expected of him. But now every village in his division claims its share of his attentions, and resents any apparent neglect.

Statesmen, then, had nothing to counteract the very natural desire of English gentlemen to escape from the dust and heat and din of the political conflict into the cooler and quieter atmosphere of country life, with all its favourite occupations.

Men like Fox and Walpole, and in our own time Lord Palmerston and Lord Derby, were able to throw off official cares when they turned their backs on Downing Street, as they took off their clothes on going to bed. But they would not have been allowed to do so now. Reproduce the old situation under our present conditions, and we should find Fox, instead of stumping the turnips after partridges, stumping the country against Jingoism, and abusing "that vile fellow," as he called Pitt, from Land's End to Berwick-upon-Tweed. Pitt would be summoned from the shades of Hollwood and his favourite pursuits at Walmer, to take the field on a similar errand. Those happy lunching-parties at the farmhouse, the huge hunches of bread and cheese, the complete freedom and *abandon*, described by Lady Hester Stanhope, would have had to be exchanged for the noisy streets of some overgrown manufacturing town, and the fetid atmosphere of town-halls and platforms. Burke would have been called away from his cows and his cottagers, and the favourite grove in which he held high converse with Windham and Johnson, to speak on behalf of the Liberal Unionists at St James's Hall or the Constitutional Club, and would have fanned the feud between himself and his former friends to frenzied exasperation. Windham would have had no time for mathematics or philosophy, and must have given up his practice of driving about from one country house to another, and conversing with all sorts and conditions of men, as was his favourite habit. These men then would have had no change. They would only have gone from one kind of Parliament to another. They would have had little time for thought, reading, and reflection; and it may be that in that case some of their finest parliamentary performances would have been lost to us. Many years ago, when this system of autumnal oratory had reached nothing like its present height, the 'Times' said in reference to a speech of Mr Disraeli's, that all work and no play made even Ben a dull boy. We may be thankful, perhaps, that men such as we have here named—the

"Magnanimi heroës, nati melioribus annis"—

were spared the ordeal.

There is a charming little picture drawn by Lockhart of a party assembled on the banks of Windermere during the last week in August 1824, at which Canning, Sir W. Scott, Professor Wilson, Wordsworth, and Southey were present, which we must transcribe *verbatim* from the Life:—

"It would have been difficult to say which star in the constellation shone with the brightest or the softest light. There was . . . a plentiful allowance, on all sides, of those airy transient pleasantries in which the fancy of poets, however wise and grave, delights to run riot when they are sure not to be misunderstood. There were beautiful and accomplished women to adorn and enjoy this circle. The weather was as Elysian as the scenery. There were brilliant cavalcades through the woods in the mornings, and delicious boatings on the lake by moonlight."

A holiday such as this is a real alterative, and when undisturbed by the necessity of replunging into the sea of politics, and preparing a big speech once a-month, would no doubt have the happiest effect in purging away the humours engendered by the parliamentary session. But a certain period of unbroken repose — a real vacation — is necessary to the beneficial effects of such recreation. And this, unfortunately, is just what our public men no longer get. Those who like it may still hunt, shoot, and fish; row with beautiful women on the lakes by moonlight; or even talk with poets and men of letters in their country houses. But they do it all under the shadow of great impending obligations, for ever bringing them back again to the same cares and anxieties, the same trains of thought, and the same moral and mental atmosphere which they have but just quitted; making that complete escape out of one life into another, that complete emancipation from political and personal worry, which is essential to curative leisure, absolutely impossible.

On the extent to which the present mode of spending the recess exhausts the health and strength of those statesmen who, with the labours of the autumnal platform, combine the responsibilities of the Cabinet Minister, it is unnecessary to dwell further. We see plainly enough, from evidence now before our eyes, that the hard work of a modern session leaves those who bear the burden and heat of the day very unfit to begin a new political campaign the moment Parliament is closed, even if it is not by itself enough to cut short their existence. That this is no fanciful or exaggerated suggestion is proved by the accompanying extract from the 'Lancet' of the 17th October 1891:—

"The remarkable and regretted deaths of two leaders of parties in one week should open the eyes of the public to the fact that only a few men are capable of bearing the strain of Parliament under the acute conditions of party strife which now obtain. It is impossible to doubt that under different conditions the lives of both Mr Smith and Mr Parnell would in all probability have been prolonged. Different hours, a different tone of public discussion, a different bearing of public men towards each other, more like that which obtains among men in common society, less heat and impulse in leaders, would alter for the better the whole character of our legislation, and would sensibly extend the lives of our best men and enable others of the sort to devote themselves to the public service. The bearing of this state of matters on the public interest should not pass unnoticed, and should encourage such rules of debate in Parliament and out, and such men only, as favour deliberation. The case of Mr Gladstone is exceptional and misleading. His *physique* is no rule for common men. He can sleep well and eat well. With all his keenness as a partisan he can withdraw himself at very short notice into another world—of philosophy, or theology, or mythology. Even for him the present strain of party life is a danger more than his friends like to think of, and from which all who admire genius and revere age would like to see him extricated. But we have to do with more ordinary mortals, on whom, in the long-run, the empire has to rely; and we repeat that for them the strain of Parliament is exhausting, and ought by all means to be abated."

If to the strain of Parliament in session is added the strain of Parliament out of session, we shall see how terribly injurious to the best interests of the public is the present system.

If such is its effect on the health of individuals, what is its effect on the health of parliamentary institutions? In these days of cheap newspapers and rapid carriage the whole country has the parliamentary debates before it every morning. It sees all that can be said on both sides of any given question by the best orators and ablest statesmen of the age. It sees their arguments discussed over again by acute and practised writers representing both political parties. Nor does this happen only once in a session. Not a single great Act of Parliament is ever carried now without the whole question being argued three or four times over, as opportunities are presented by different stages of the bill. On each occasion the press repeats its comments, readjusts the facts and figures, sets forth the premises and enforces the conclusions anew, till at last it can only be the man who is wholly indifferent to the subject who does not know all that can be known about it. Now, what is the inevitable result of beginning this process all over again—speeches, leading articles, and all—as soon as Parliament is prorogued? Can it fail to weary and disgust the public with the very name of politics? They *must* get sick of the forced invective, the threadbare topics, the hackneyed gibes and sarcasms served up to them by our itinerant politicians between September and January. And what is the further consequence of their becoming sick and tired of such stuff? It is this, that they gradually come to listen to or to read such orations not for anything to be learned from them, but simply as so many exhibitions of party pluck and vigour, and as tests of the capacity of their respective champions for winning the great stake. They come to look on a good speech as a lover of the ring in old times looked on a well-fought round by the pugilist whom he had backed to win. Thus Parliament out of session is simply a big gladiatorial show. This is all it is good for. Statesmanship, political principle, great public and imperial interests, are dragged down to this level, and rolled in the mire to make sport for the audience. The system, in a word, cheapens and degrades politics to such a degree, that we can hardly wonder at the slight effect which is now very often produced by appeals to more elevated considerations. A feeling of general satiety, of indifference and languor, mingled with one of growing contempt and dislike for popular and parliamentary institutions, if they necessitate such scenes as these, is gradually diffused through the community, undermining its political energies and sapping its political faith, till public spirit may become so torpid as to make any kind of revolution possible.

People are fond of asking why nobody reads the

debates now. The answer is simple. They have read them all before. And what is still more to the purpose is, that our parliamentary orators have spoken them all before. The future is discounted as well as the past repeated by these hard-pressed disputants. The public bring a jaded appetite to a stale banquet. Formerly, when Parliament met, there was some public curiosity to be satisfied. All was new. Eloquence had again become a novelty. The rivals met in the arena with recruited vigour and sharpened rhetoric, with a fresh store of arguments, images, and epigrams, to elevate and to embellish their discourse. Then the debates sparkled. Then it was an intellectual treat to read through four or five columns of the morning papers. But now all the life is taken out of the debates before they begin. It is impossible for any man to be at his best when he is only repeating in Parliament what he has been saying all over the country for the last three months, and which everybody knows by heart. This is one great secret of the flatness and dulness in the parliamentary debates of which everybody now complains. Parliament out of session is the ruin of Parliament in session. The House of Commons gradually loses ground in public estimation, through no fault in its constitution, but merely because on the shoulders of its leading men a burden is laid greater than they can bear. "It was always the trick of our English nation," says Falstaff, "when they had got a good thing, to make it too common."

Finally, we have to consider what is, or probably will be, the effect on politics of making public life a business to which men have to apply themselves the whole year round, as they do to the bar, to the exchange, or the factory. Again, the answer to this question is one which he who runs may read. Professional politics will be left to professional politicians —men who enter Parliament intending to live by it, as they would by the practice of law, medicine, or commerce. This system would, of course, very soon lead to the payment of members, and it would not stop there. An income derived from this source would be extremely precarious, and could only be regarded by professional politicians as a stepping-stone to something better. Thus the number of men in

Parliament who wanted something from the Government would be enormously increased, and the independence of the House, as a body, be proportionally diminished. Even if we set aside, for the moment, mere pecuniary considerations, we shall see that, under the conditions we are supposing, the character of the House must necessarily deteriorate. The class of men we are contemplating, if they were not paid in coin, would want to be paid in cake; if they did not want place, they would certainly want something else. They would not give their time and trouble for nothing. They would want celebrity, notoriety, or whatever else it might be called. Thus the number of members who desired always "to keep themselves in evidence," as the phrase runs, large as it is now, would then be still larger; and the House of Commons, unmanageable as it is now, would then be more intractable than ever.

Now the majority of the country gentlemen who sit in the House of Commons accept a seat in Parliament as one of the natural duties appertaining to their station in life,—a dignified and honourable duty, no doubt, but not one which many of them would care to undertake for the sake of any personal gratification it affords them. It is simply one out of many obligations which their position imposes on them. They have to manage their estates, to look after their tenantry, to attend to local business, to help in the maintenance of law and order, and also at stated times to give their attendance in the great council of the nation, to watch over the wider interests of the entire empire. Formerly almost every Royal Speech on the prorogation of Parliament referred to the important duties awaiting members of Parliament in their respective counties. In Parliament they make their influence felt in a quiet, unobtrusive manner, and not only bring to bear on the debates that knowledge of business and practical acquaintance with administrative duties to which they are trained from their boyhood, but contribute also, in a very great degree, to maintain a high tone of feeling and a high standard of honour in the popular assembly. But they do not care to make long speeches, to see their names continually in the newspapers, or to have a hand in every question that comes before the House, whatever its character or magnitude. Neither their vanity nor their ambition offers any obstruction to public business, though there may be a few fighting men among them, who, for the mere fun of the thing, for the *gaudium certaminis,* occasionally distinguish themselves in this branch of parliamentary warfare. But it is not the habit of the class.

On the greater number of these men — not, of course, on all — the threat of a dissolution falls harmlessly. To be out of Parliament does not make them less important. Their position in society is assured; and if their constituents reject them, though they may be mortified for the moment by the loss of confidence which it implies, they have abundant compensations to which the professional politician is a stranger. We ask any impartial man whether Parliament would lose or gain by the withdrawal from the House of Commons of the former class, leaving their places to be filled up by the latter. If politics become a trade, the House of Commons will become a shop Principles and projects will be turned over like bales of muslin or samples of grocery, and puffed and pressed upon the public according to the return they promise. Try our disestablishment at so much; taste our Home Rule; compulsory abstinence very cheap to-day; and so on. This is what politics would in time be brought to in the hands of professional politicians.

The tendency of our present system, the recess as it is, is certainly in this direction. It cannot be expected that the gentry as a class should continue to give their unpaid services to the nation if the nation in return leaves them no leisure to enjoy themselves in their own way, which is all the remuneration they ask. It may be said, of course, if the country gentlemen don't choose to take the trouble to come to Parliament to look after their own interests, they cannot expect other people to do it for them. If they don't choose to sacrifice their leisure and their country life to the public good, the public will soon leave them no pleasures to enjoy, and more leisure than they want. It may be so; but though this would punish the gentry, it would not bring them back to the House of Commons; and we are now considering what the country, not what the gentry, would lose by such a change. The time would come, we think, when even many honest Radicals would be obliged to admit that a Parliament of professional place-hunters and lovers of notoriety at any price was a bad exchange, after all, for the squirearchy, who, with all their faults, were at least men of practical common-sense, experienced in business, and inaccessible to bribes; who did their duty without fussing and foaming or making mountains out of mole-hills; and who had the advantage, as Mr Chamberlain himself has admitted, of being gentlemen.

No change in either the length or the season of the recess would necessarily affect the abuse of it which we have here been considering. But changes have been proposed for other reasons, and they are these: first, in the hope that a longer session may overpower the system of obstruction; secondly, because there is a growing dislike in the House of Commons to sitting so late into the summer. It is doubtful, however, whether any enlargement of the session would by itself be sufficient to nullify such obstruction as we have recently witnessed. The obstructionists would be equal to the occasion, and could spin out their system as a spider does its web, out of their own bowels, to any length that was necessary. On the second plea there is more to be said, but it is a question which is complicated by many conflicting considerations. We cannot go back to the old system exactly as it was, and hardly any alternative can be suggested which will not inconvenience somebody.

The more the recess becomes like another session, and the more the session encroaches on the sphere of the recess, the greater the risk we run of altering the composition of the House of Commons in the manner now described. Yet it ought to be perfectly possible so to redistribute the time now usually allotted to the session, and even to extend it, as not seriously to interrupt either the duties or the pleasures of a class so essential to the efficiency of Parliament as the English landed proprietor. It has been proposed that the session should terminate in the beginning of July, and begin at the end of October. To repeat what we have said, the time proposed is not long enough, and it falls at the wrong season of the year. It is not long enough for two reasons,—first, because it would not bring the requisite period of relief to our overworked statesmen; and secondly, because, as has been pointed out by highly competent critics, it is contrary to the public good that the Executive should be constantly exposed to the harrowing process of parliamentary interrogation and the noisome buzz of political bluebottles for more than half the year. A system which was originally intended for the detection of abuses has now become an abuse itself, by which the principle of Government is continually corroded, its authority lessened, and its dignity degraded; and to enlarge the period within which these practices are possible would be the most cruel unkindness we could inflict on representative institutions.

A recess from midsummer to Michaelmas would fall at the wrong time of the year for two reasons likewise. If it be thought a small thing that it would rob so many members of both Houses of those healthy and invigorating rural sports in which they now forget the asperities of party warfare, and recruit their physical strength after six months spent in the exhausting atmosphere of Parliament, it cannot be thought a small thing that it should curtail, if it did not entirely destroy, all their opportunities of mixing freely with the farmers and labourers of the county. A recess which began with the beginning of the hay harvest and ended with the end of the corn harvest, would be exactly coextensive with the very busiest period of the year both for the farmer and the labourer; and just when they became at leisure to attend meetings, agricultural shows, and other gatherings which bring the rural population together, their parliamentary representatives would be called away to their duties in another place. The hours of attendance in the session are regulated with a view to one large class of members who have business engagements elsewhere—namely, the lawyers; and due regard should also be shown to the convenience of another class who have duties scarcely less important. I am not called upon to decide positively when the session should end and when it should begin.

There must always be a margin, either for contraction or expansion. But the six months which begin with the 1st of August seem at all events either the right time for the recess, or the right time out of which to carve the recess.

We have little real summer in England now before the middle of July; and if Parliament were prorogued at the end of that month to meet again the first week in January, nobody would lose much in the article either of summer suns or autumn sports. If, for the sake of the Christmas holidays, we took the first fortnight in December instead of the first fortnight in January, members of Parliament would have August, September, October, and November at their absolute disposal, with half December and half January as well, which would give them as much time for travelling, fishing, shooting, and hunting as they could reasonably desire, independently of the many off-days which they are always able to secure. Such an arrangement would leave the country gentlemen two clear months between the end of the harvest and the meeting of Parliament to move about among their constituents and discharge all those other public duties to which we have referred; and the general system of English rural life, with all its habits, customs, and traditions, would remain untouched.

The duration of the session, with the season at which it should be fixed, is a separate question from that with which this chapter commences— namely, the most useful and beneficial mode of spending it. The dedication of the parliamentary holiday to what may be called work out of school has been carried to an excess which is mischievous to all parties concerned in it. Our senators should play when they are at play, and work when they are at work. And the vast majority of the public would be exceedingly thankful to see the newspapers filled during the autumn with something more amusing than eight or ten columns of extra-parliamentary speeches. The principal London morning papers have almost entirely lost their old literary character. We look in vain in the 'Times' for those admirable reviews of books which, down to twenty years ago, were so attractive a feature in the leading journal. The 'Standard' never gave quite so much space to literary matter, but what it did give it has taken away. And the answer is always the same. It is blocked out by the big speeches of vacation orators. Formerly, when Parliament was up, a number of columns were at once set free for more lively and entertaining matter. Now, it is the same dull tale of politics and party warfare the whole year round. To shorten the recess would only aggravate the evil. If we must bear with the prolongation of political loquacity all through the autumn—and it seems too firmly established now to be got rid of—let us submit to it in patience rather than fly for refuge to the worse offender of the two. The recess may bore us, but in Parliament we see agencies at work fraught with ruin alike to representative institutions and to social liberty.

Obstruction, if it cannot be suppressed, cannot be allowed to be the prerogative of a single party. If one side chooses to make legislation impossible for its opponents, the other side will do so too. Conservatives cannot have their own failures imputed to incompetence, and the successes of the Radicals to superior ability, when, were the same tactics employed against the Radicals as the Radicals employ against the Conservatives, the result would be exactly the same. That can never be permitted; yet hardly a single politician in his sober senses would deny that a few more sessions like that of 1890 would bring parliamentary government and our existing constitution within measurable distance of their end.

I would, moreover, venture to suggest that the operation of this system is gradually teaching the people something. It is teaching them that this informal and irregular political agency, though it cannot legislate, can do almost everything else which Parliament can do. It can drag abuses into the light of publicity. It can expose or circulate fallacies, as the case may be, with equal facility and effect. It can bring the influence of public opinion to bear on the policy of Ministers or the conduct of the Opposition with equal force and almost equal directness. It can explain or obscure measures, perplex or simplify public questions, with as much clearness and adroitness. If we are told that, true as this may be, it is only true because the orators of the recess *are* members of Parliament, and that if they were not, half they say would be unheeded,—the answer is that it would not be so if there were no Parliament at all, and no man had any advantage over another in that respect. Now, of course, a member of Parliament, especially if he is a member of the Government, or one of the Opposition leaders, speaks with an authority to which no private man can make pretence. But if no comparison of this kind were possible, and all spoke from the outside, would not the same qualities which bring a man to the front in Parliament bring him to the front on the platform, and would not real eloquence, political knowledge, and great intellectual power, command as ready attention as they do now? We are drawing no conclusions, but such reflections must naturally occur to us as we contemplate the oratory of the autumn. The House of Commons is no longer the sole guardian of our liberties and our persons. It is no longer the sole or the most effective critic of Ministerial policy, whether foreign or domestic. Its natural child shows a vigour and ability not uncommon to illegitimate offspring. The two together give us too much of a good thing, and are likely to make us tired of both. This can hardly last for ever—one of the two must retire from the field. It is even now fast coming to be recognised that either the "recess as it is" or the session as it is, involves a great waste of force, and too great a strain both on the health and strength of politicians and the interest and attention of the public. What will happen if England ever becomes really and thoroughly tired of political discussion, we forbear to conjecture. But it is an experiment which the leading class of politicians seem bent on trying. We fully admit the difficulty of making any change now, for who is to stop first? The disease, we fear, must run its course, and we must await the result with what fortitude we may.

THE FARMERS.

THE word "farmer" is a much more comprehensive one at the present day than it used to be in former times. It was once applied almost exclusively to the class of men which, according to its derivation, it properly denotes—those, that is, who till hired ground, as distinct from the yeoman, or, later on, the gentleman farmer, who tills his own. Within the last generation, however, the love of agriculture has spread so widely among all classes, that tenant-farmers may now be found in every rank of society. Yet even now, the word, taken simply by itself, without any differentiating term, is usually held to signify one who stands below the line conventionally supposed to separate the "table-land of gentility," as Mr Oldbuck calls it, from all beneath. That is the sense in which I propose to use it on the present occasion. Distinctions of this nature are always more or less invidious; nor should I have mentioned them at all, but for the necessity of making perfectly clear to what manner of man I was referring. Not to pursue this question any further, it is obvious that among agriculturists in general, whether amateurs or professionals, the line of demarcation is a very irregular and devious one; and I shall content myself with saying that in writing of the manners, the prejudices, the habits, the vices and virtues of this particular class, whether yeomen or tenants, I am throughout referring to men who have not, as a rule, received a liberal education, and who do not, or did not till within the last thirty years, think of copying the manners and customs pertaining to the class above them.

I say this with the less hesitation, because it will rather be to what are called " farmers of the old school" that I shall direct attention, affording, as they do, the most strongly marked types of the genus to which they belong, and illustrating most clearly that old tripartite division of rural life which I believe is peculiar to this country, and which, with some inconveniences, has hitherto worked most beneficially. But whether dealing with the old style or new, I shall be thinking chiefly of the man who occupies a middle position between the peasant farmer and the gentleman farmer, or the tenant who is socially his equal; neither of these two extremes being equally characteristic of England, or exhibiting in the same perfection the traits on which I love to look back. There are peasant farmers and gentlemen farmers everywhere. But the man I have in my eye is only to be found at home.

My own recollections go back to a time when there were still a good many farmers left who lived quite *more majorum*—dined in their kitchens, drank nothing but ale, and were only just beginning to take to black coats on Sunday. One such man I can remember well, who has indeed not been dead for more than ten or twelve years. He was the sole surviving specimen in the neighbourhood where he lived of a class which had been long extinct, and was pointed out by other farmers as a social curiosity. But he was a warm man, had a large balance at his bankers, and kept his farm, some 300 acres, in excellent condition, albeit little indebted to science or machinery. He was a kind of king on market-days, for whatever he bought, he would always have the best, and never haggled at the price. If you called upon him, he received you in the kitchen, and a jug of home-brewed, that incomparable luxury which has almost disappeared before the march of refinement, was placed upon the table, with no apology for not offering wine. He never missed church, and could always be relied upon when money was wanted for any charitable or religious purpose. He, we may be sure, was never behind-hand with his rent, nor ever asked for a reduction. His farm was a sufficient occupation for him. He neither shot nor hunted, though he had opportunities of doing both. He had no books: and though not possessed of high spirits or a man of many words, was always cheerful, always sober, and always ceremoniously respectful to those whom he recognised as his betters. When he died, it was found that he had amassed money; and though he lived into the bad times, he did not seem to have suffered from them.

Another of the same kind, whom I remember still better, was a somewhat crabbed and gnarled old fellow, but thoroughly sound at core. I can just recollect him at church, dressed a good deal like Mr Poyser—the same drab coat and breeches, and the same richly flowered waistcoat. These, however, disappeared in my early childhood, about the same time as the village stocks and the parish clerk's top-boots, and gave way to the broad-skirted black garment which remained his Sunday attire to his death. The sons of such men were then wearing swallow-tailed coats, generally dark-green or brown, with brass buttons. But the fathers remained faithful to the old style, and I think, as far as personal appearance went, they had the best of it. Old Master Woollem, as he was always called —his real name was Woolcome — was a man of saturnine temperament, disliked rather by us boys because he objected to our getting over his fences, or prowling about his farmyard and out-houses, bird-nesting, or sparrow-catching; but a staunch friend to the parson, an excellent master, and liberal in his charities. He was even more strict in his devotion to old farming ideas than the other old gentleman I have mentioned. He had been brought up at a time when farmers or their wives and daughters went off to market in the winter while it was still dark, transacted their business by candle-light, and were home again by dinner-time. To the last he did not like to see his daughters doing any ornamental work, reading any light literature, or exhibiting the faintest approach to any little finery in their dress. If he detected anything of the kind, he generally remained quite silent, but those who knew him knew well what he meant. Sometimes he refused food—literally, like David, turning his face to the wall and eating no bread. The last authenticated instance of his declining to eat his dinner was on his suddenly discovering that his eldest son had been guilty of a breach of all the family traditions by going out with the hounds.

The young man did not appear at table. The new spurs were missing from their accustomed hook over the fireplace. The old man remembered that the hounds had met in the neighbourhood that morning. The bitter truth flashed upon him in a moment. "My lord's gone a-hunting," he exclaimed to his wife, with suppressed emotion, "and you knowed to it." This last reflection was too much for him, and, drawing his chair away to the chimney-corner, he refused to be comforted. His silence on these occasions was more terrible than words: he moved about the house and premises wrapped in the deepest gloom: and during one of these fits of dejection, his youngest daughter, a nice-looking girl of nineteen, was driven in despair to tuck up her sleeves, go down upon her knees, and scrub the kitchen-floor till her arms ached, as the only means of recalling him to more cheerful views of existence. Propitiated by this act of homage to the spirit of a better age and the deities of his own youth, old Master Woollem is said to have actually smiled, and harmony was once more restored to the domestic circle.

In spite of these little peculiarities, Woolcome was a man of great natural shrewdness and general intelligence, was never loud or noisy in his talk, and knew "how to conduct himself," and what kind of language to use, in whatever society he was thrown. He would never have said the gross things which some farmers of those days uttered quite innocently concerning their flocks and herds, nor yet the really simple or really racy things which I have heard from others, indicating no doubt some confusion of ideas, but all the more interesting on that account to students of the laws of thought.

I recollect a great, big, burly fellow, six feet high, and younger than either of the above, who, when asked his age, could only refer the questioner to his landlord. "I am three years younger nor Sir Richard," he would say; "I allers wos." This was conclusive in his eyes. I once saw this man trembling on the verge of scepticism in consequence of the inexplicable behaviour of the elements. That a heavy flood should have come on the day after he had brought down his sheep from the uplands, and turned them into the meadows, was more than he could reconcile with the theory of a moral governor of the universe. "It seemed very odd," he said; and I left him leaning on a gate struggling very hard to vindicate the ways of God to man, but evidently without success. This man ultimately hanged himself in his stable — whether distracted by the difficulties surrounding the origin of evil, or vexed, as the neighbours thought, at being cheated out of the price of a calf, I have never fully understood.

These were all men of the old leaven—men who, if not free from the vices and deficiencies common to the middle classes in general, possessed at least some negative virtues peculiar to themselves. They were neither luxurious nor ostentatious; were content to live after the manner of their forefathers, and had no desire to be anything but what they were. Their only vehicle was the old "shay-cart"; and very few of them hunted, unless they were breeders of, or dealers in, horses, and did it professionally. They farmed well according to the fashion of the age, and had no other ambition. They lived very plainly, not to say hardly — by no means thinking it necessary to eat butcher's meat every day. I knew a thriving farmer, renting two hundred acres — which, in the midland counties, is considered a good-sized farm — and keeping forty cows, who sat down with his family every Sunday to a large batter-pudding made in a puncheon, with a piece of bacon in the middle, which they ate cold for dinner during the remainder of the week. The cost of living to farmers of this class was a mere trifle. They bought scarcely anything. Milk, butter, cheese, bacon, eggs, poultry, pork, and vegetables, they got at cost price off their own land. They brewed their own beer and baked their own bread. Families who lived much better than those who assembled round the puncheon — our friend Woollem, for instance — couldn't have spent more than three hundred a-year, and I don't suppose he spent that. Suppose his farm was three hundred acres, and that he paid £2 an acre for it all round: according to the common calculation in those days,[1] his land would yield him three

---

[1] Not in these. See a most interesting paper read by Major Craigie before the Farmers' Club in London on December 10, 1888, "The Farmers' Labour Bill."

rents — one for his landlord, one for his labour, and one for himself. That would give him £600 a-year for his own share. I believe that if anything I am under the mark, for some said the tenant should make four rents, one to put by, besides what I have mentioned. But allowing the first calculation to be correct, a thrifty man, in the days I am thinking of, would have saved between three and four hundred a-year; and this very old man we have been talking about—Woolcome—did actually die worth some £15,000, besides the value of his stock, having had the farm for forty years. This was the generation that made money; the next was the generation that spent it; the present is the one that wants it.

There have, of course, always been, coexistent with the above class of farmers, a higher and a lower class. The farmer who rented, maybe, seven or eight hundred acres, and had land of his own besides, though not perhaps a gentleman any more than the men I have described, was a man of different tastes and habits, hunted and shot, and sometimes went to the seaside. On the other hand, the smaller man with thirty, fifty, or seventy acres, was little more than a peasant. But I think the class which came between the two was, as I have already said, the most truly representative; and this is the class, I am afraid, on whom "time and fate" have laid the heaviest hand. But they could not, under any circumstances, have remained as they were forty years ago. The march of intellect must have gone over them, flattening down their characteristic oddities and removing their moss-grown prejudices, even had no agricultural depression threatened to extinguish them. Such men may doubtless still be found unchanged in the remoter nooks and corners of the country. I have heard that they survive in Devonshire; but they are fast disappearing from the great agricultural counties in the central and eastern parts of England. Were the present writer to outlive them all, he could never forget them — their kindly, hearty ways, their homely politeness and hospitality, their mellow ale and their pork-pies, produced, generally speaking, on coursing days, that being a sport in which the most scrupulous of them thought it no presumption to indulge.

"Saturnia regna, valete."

If another golden age is in store for us, I at all events shall not be here to see it.

Between the smaller yeomen and the tenant-farmer such as I have described him, there was never much to choose in point of intelligence, education, or refinement. The small freeholders once upon a time, perhaps, were a valuable political element in rural society, and to some extent they are so still. But everybody in the country is tolerably independent now, and the old-fashioned yeoman, with his many real and many imputed virtues, mingled so large an infusion of more questionable qualities, that I know not whether his gradual disappearance is altogether to be regretted. Not that he has disappeared yet, by any means. "People ask," said Lord Beaconsfield, " where the Buckinghamshire freeholders are now? Why, where you would expect to find them—in Buckinghamshire, to be sure." And it is a great mistake to suppose that the class of small proprietors has either vanished or is likely to vanish very soon. They are not subject to the same disturbing causes as the tenant-farmer. The owner may farm as badly as he pleases, exhaust his land, allow his house, his farm-buildings, and his fences to go to rack and ruin; but as long as he can scrape enough from the soil to pay the interest on his mortgage and keep body and soul together, there is nobody to move him on. As we know, he clings tenaciously to the ground, and the result is that he is still there when many better men than himself have been obliged to go. His time may come, as it would assuredly come, in the third or fourth generation, to any new class of peasant-proprietors. But he is not yet a thing of the past, and is still to be seen, in a state of nature, in all the English counties that I am acquainted with. I may here add that, according to the latest agricultural returns, of the thirty-two million seven hundred thousand acres of which England consists, very nearly five millions are farmed by their owners.

The peasant-proprietor was and is simply what his name implies. It was and is the yeoman of two or three hundred acres in whom the special attributes of his class are seen to the greatest perfection. In a country village of the olden time, with no resident gentleman, such a man was under no moral restraint whatever. There was no public opinion, and if there had been, he would not have cared about it. He was a little king—as irresponsible and despotic as a Turkish pasha. A good type of the class has been given us by George Eliot in Squire Cass. He was rather above the yeoman class in point of property. But his character was exactly theirs. Such men, generally speaking, did not, and do not, set a good example to the neighbourhood. They were, as a rule, scrupulously honest, liberal, and hospitable. But as for temperance, soberness, and chastity, these virtues were whistled down the wind. Twenty years ago they were still very much what the smallest class of squires had been a hundred and fifty years before. There were good men and moral men among them then, and probably there are more now. But their absolute freedom from the corrective influence of all outside opinion; their ignorance and self-importance; their well-filled pockets, and their limited range of interests,—betrayed too many of them into the same mode of living as Tony Lumpkin promised himself when he should "come to his own."

Even the most old-fashioned farmers whom I can recollect had given up the practice of dining with their labourers. They no longer sat at the head of the long oak-table and carved the bacon, as Cobbett remembered them doing; and even in his day the process of transformation had begun. In 1825 he wrote as follows:—

"When the old farm-houses are down (and down they must come in time), what a miserable thing the country will be! Those that are now erected are mere painted shells, with a mistress within who is so stuck up in a place she calls the *parlour*, with, if she have children, the 'young ladies and gentlemen' about her; some showy chairs and a sofa (a *sofa* by all means); half-a-dozen prints in gilt frames hanging up; some swinging book-shelves with novels and tracts upon them; a dinner brought in by a girl that is perhaps better 'educated' than she; two or three nicknacks to eat instead of a piece of bacon and a pudding; the house too neat for a dirty-shoed carter to be allowed to come into; and everything proclaiming to every sensible beholder that there is here a constant anxiety to make a *show* not warranted by the reality. The children (which is the worst part of it) are all too clever to *work*; they are all to be *gentlefolks*. Go to plough! Good God! What! 'young gentlemen' go to plough! They become *clerks*, or some skimming-dish thing or other. They flee from the dirty *work* as cunning horses do from the bridle. What misery is all this! What a mass of materials for proclaiming that general and *dreadful convulsion* that must, first or last, come and blow this funding and jobbing and enslaving and starving system to atoms!"[1]

Cobbett was riding through the home counties when he wrote this, and sixty years ago the change had hardly spread a great deal farther. Still this was the beginning of it, and we likewise read on the same page—

"There was no reason to expect that farmers would not endeavour to keep pace, in point of show and luxury, with fund-holders, and with all the tribe that *war* and *taxes* created. Farmers were not the authors of the mischief. And *now* they are compelled to shut the labourers out of their houses, and to pinch them in their wages in order

---

[1] Rural Rides and Drives, p. 274.

to be able to pay their own taxes; and besides this, the manners and the principles of the working class are so changed, that a sort of self-preservation bids the farmer (especially in some counties) to keep them from beneath his roof."[1]

The distress among the peasantry which caused this last sentence to be written passed away in time. But the change in the farmers went on, and in the course of another generation produced the new race of whose style of living we have heard so much since the agricultural depression set in. Cobbett's picture, which I have here quoted, represents the change under its most ridiculous aspect; and as events have turned out, it proved an unfortunate one for the farmers. Had they continued to live in the old style during what have been called the good times—that is to say, roughly speaking, from about 1835 to 1875—they might have been in a very different position now. It took nearly twenty years for things to settle down again after the peace of 1815; but as soon as the farmers had got over the monetary convulsions of the Regency and the reign of George IV.,

[1] Rural Rides and Drives, p. 274.

a period of great prosperity followed, and it was the younger generation of farmers, who grew up to manhood about the middle of the present century, with whom the luxuries and elegancies so severely censured by a somewhat inconsiderate class of critics originated. I cannot altogether join in these reproaches. The smart dog-cart, the well-bred hunter, the claret, the piano, the governess, the silk dresses, and the last new novel, were not reprehensible in themselves. There is no reason why men should not have these things, simply because they are agriculturists; and if the farmers fell into the error of supposing that their good fortune would last for ever, and that there was no necessity to make provision for a rainy day, they only did what many other people of various occupations and pursuits in life are guilty of doing every hour, without drawing down upon themselves any marked sarcasm or censure. It might be said, perhaps, that all classes in England have been living too expensively during the last fifty years, and that country gentlemen are paying the penalty of their imprudence as well as their tenants.

The tenant-farmer of the new style has been so

often described, that it is unnecessary to paint him over again in any detail. He "set up for a gentleman," as the labourers used to say, and played the part with varying propriety, according to his natural tact and taste, and the kind of education he had received. The degree in which he succeeded in raising himself towards the level of the class above him would depend to some extent, of course, on the character of the neighbourhood in which he lived, and the number and quality of the gentry who took the lead in it. But it would be a mistake to suppose that all the young farmers who, five-and-thirty or forty years ago, began to ride valuable horses, drink expensive wines, and smoke choice cigars, did so with the view of making themselves more like gentlemen. The majority of them, I think, had too much sense for that. They had these things because they were good in themselves, and they saw no reason for hoarding their money instead of spending it. But of that social ambition which is said to agitate mercantile and commercial circles, I have never myself seen much evidence among the farmers. They were quite contented, I think, with the society of their own class, and acquiesced in existing distinctions not only without any irritation, but without the slightest desire to rebel against them.

In one particular this was very marked. Let us go to the cover-side and take a glance at the assembled sportsmen. There is the gentleman on his handsome hunter, with perfect appointments; his boots and buckskins, his scarlet coat, his tie, his pin, all exactly as they ought to be. Talking to him is a good-looking young man, nearly if not quite as well mounted as himself, and nearly if not quite as well dressed. He is quite as good a rider, and the fox to-day will in all probability be found upon his own farm. But there is a line drawn between them which the latter knows to be impassable. He cannot wear a red coat. He would like to wear one, and would no doubt look very well in one. But he knows perfectly well that "it wouldn't do,"—that it would only make him look ridiculous; and he never frets or chafes for a moment under a dispensation which seems to him like a natural law. Similarly, I don't believe that such men have ever pined for admittance into what is called "county society," either for themselves, their wives, or their daughters; and when we hear them accused of having aped a style of living unsuitable to their position, and of having given themselves airs for which now they have to pay the piper, we must remember, after all, that in the majority of instances they only intended to enjoy themselves, and were not chargeable, as a rule, with any contemptible eagerness to thrust themselves into a higher class. When the rustic said of such a man that he was "setting up for a gentleman," he was sarcastic, and meant that he would have done much better to spend less upon himself, and more upon his land and his labourers' wages. He did not necessarily mean that the culprit was looking forward to an invitation to dinner from the Duke, or an alliance with his landlord's daughter.

We are now speaking of men whose fathers, grandfathers, and great-grandfathers had been farmers before them—men who were thoroughly imbued with all the traditions of their class, and perfectly satisfied with the social conditions which surrounded them. But of course there were others. The system of farming-pupils has something perhaps to answer for. It used to be said that the fool of the family was sent into the army. That is not the case now, if it ever was. But though I do not mean to say that parents often resolved to make the fool of the family a farmer, I think they sometimes fancied that a boy who either could or would do nothing else, might be bribed to work a little at farming by the prospect which it afforded him of good living, an out-of-door life, and plenty of field-sports. Nine times out of ten the lad took all the fun and shirked all the work, and was probably no very good companion for the young farmers in the neighbourhood. They acquired expensive tastes and idle habits from *him*; while his agricultural tutor, who received an ample fee with him, made it a point of honour to keep what was called "a liberal table," and to indulge in luxuries which, if left to himself, he would have thought beyond his station. The farmer's wife was specially fond of this system; for if she had daughters, the pupil would naturally take one of them off her hands, and she in turn would send others to do the same kind office for her sisters.

Occasionally such families got rather a bad reputation in the neighbourhood, and the labourers would tell you with a grin how young So-and-so "got zucked in" by Farmer Plant's lady at the Grange. "Be you a-gooing to stay there?" perhaps he would add; and if you answered in the affirmative, would grin a little wider. If you asked him what he meant, he would only say, "Well, you'll 'ev to be smart like." The pupil business, however, is now said to be played out.[1] Men don't send their sons, even the idle ones, to learn a losing trade at a large cost; and what is gradually becoming of the tutorial farmers, with their horses and guns, their elegant daughters and their late dinners, I do not profess to understand. Some still remain, I suppose, but in too many places vacant farms and empty farmhouses, and gardens overgrown with weeds, tell plainly that their day is over; and that the age of pleasure-farming—of work and play combined in very unequal proportions—is gone for ever.

[1] See an excellent article in the 'St James's Gazette,' October 26, 1889.

One is very sorry for individuals; but I am not sure that the catastrophe which has overtaken them is an unmixed evil. There was something artificial in the social efflorescence of the agricultural class during what has been called the champagne age. I have already pointed out that much of the sarcasm to which farmers have been exposed, in consequence of the tastes and habits then acquired, is undeserved; that, in fact, they have not been worse than other people. But at the same time, their prosperity depended upon two conditions, one of which was always precarious, while it might have been seen that the other was in the nature of things only temporary—I mean, the existence of Protection and the absence of competition. The withdrawal of the one, followed at no long interval by the extension of the other, has produced its logical results. Some say that protection, in some shape or another, is sure to be revived; others that, in less than another generation, American competition, at all events, will cease to be formidable. But it can hardly help occurring to any impartial looker-on that it would be better for all parties if English agriculture could be placed on such a footing as would make it independent of either. This is what I should call a natural and healthy footing. I am not writing either as a political economist or a scientific agriculturist; but I think common-sense is enough to teach us this, that if the style of living adopted by a numerous class of English farmers during the second half of the nineteenth century requires to be supported by laws to which a large part of the nation would always be hostile, and is incompatible with that foreign competition which, though it may possibly subside at some remote period, must continue to confront us for very many years to come, the sooner it is exchanged for a system that can dispense with such supports the better.

Of the actual economical position of the English farmer at the present moment, it is impossible to procure the details with sufficient accuracy to warrant any lengthened description. It seems to be generally admitted that he can no longer continue to live in the style to which he has lately grown accustomed; and the great question is, whether he can continue to live at all upon the land, even if he returns to that simpler and more frugal mode of life which prevailed at a much earlier period? On the answer to this question it depends whether the tenant-farmer is still to continue a conspicuous and important member of the village community, a link between the gentry and the peasantry, of which the value in past times has been incalculable; or whether he is gradually to fade out of the system, leaving the land to the aristocracy and the peasantry, to be cultivated either on a larger scale by the former, or on a smaller scale by the latter.

After the many changes which our old rural life has already undergone, and in view of the many more which it yet seems doomed to undergo, the disappearance of the middle-class tenant-farmer from among the constituent elements of rural society cannot, I fear, be regarded as impossible. But I confess I do not think it probable. It does not seem to me that the wholesale substitution of petty culture, whether by the hands of owners or occupiers, for our existing agricultural system, leaving no intermediate link between the peasantry and the gentry, is within measurable distance. An American agriculturist said to me but a few months ago,—" Why, put down an American farmer on two hundred acres of clay land in your Cambridgeshire or Essex, at a pound an acre, and he would not only make a living out of it—he would grow rich upon it." And I think it has certainly not yet been proved that if the occupier of two or three hundred acres returned to the style of living which was universal among men of his class in the reign of George II., and till the middle of the reign of George III., they could not live upon the land. The style of living among the gentry must be altered too: the two classes must lower their expenditure together. Eight thousand a-year must come back to five, and five thousand a-year to three. And though I do not presume to speak with confidence of the result, yet I think it will be owned that the experiment has not yet been tried upon a large scale, and that it is worth a trial. Rents, of course, have in numerous instances been remitted or reduced. But country gentlemen must make up their minds to a permanently different mode of life, if the old distribution of classes is to remain intact. In that case, I think, with a homelier and less showy class of tenantry, and a class of gentry retaining all their culture while parting with some of their luxuries, country life might still be conducted on the old model, in spite of county councils—which, it is hoped, will disappoint the Radicals — and other plausible nostrums, which they might perhaps turn to better account.

That it may be so, I for one most heartily and earnestly desire. Let us try to picture to ourselves an England from which the tenant-farmers—not only the Woolcomes and their like, but their modern representatives—had disappeared. Let us try to think of English villages in which the half-dozen substantial farmhouses, with the comfortable farmyards, barns, and ricks, were no longer to be seen; of the village church, from which the old well-known figures of Farmer Giles, and Farmer Goodman, and Farmer Whitehead, were gone for ever. None but those who know what an English village of the old stamp really is, will perhaps fully appreciate all that these words imply. In the first place, they mean the loss of a body of men who have hitherto taken a large share in the administration of local affairs, and for whom it would be difficult to find efficient substitutes. If the present race of farmers vanish, and in their place we have only a multitude of petty cultivators, with a few very big agriculturists scattered about here and there—the plums at the top of the pudding—who is to assist the gentry and the clergy in the conduct of country business? The electors, in the case we are supposing, will be obliged to choose the attorney and the shopkeeper from the nearest town, in default of anybody else with the requisite education and intelligence—men ignorant of rural matters, and of the real wants and true interests of the peasantry. More than that, parish affairs will have to be managed by somebody. Neither county councils nor district councils will do away with the necessity for that; and who is to manage them if there are no farmers in the parish above the rank of a peasant?

But the man who would miss the farmers most

of all would be the clergyman. There are farmers who are Dissenters, and a few who, being such, do all they can to thwart the parson. But, as a general rule, the principal farmers in the parish are the clergyman's most efficient helpers. They are independent men, and speak their minds about ritualism, or anything else which offends them, with perfect freedom. But a man of this kind is often the clergyman's right-hand man for all that, subscribes liberally to the school, looks after the Church-rate, and helps to keep up what is called "a good feeling" in the parish generally. He takes a good deal of parish business off the parson's hands, helps him in works of charity, carries coal for the poor at Christmas, and can often give useful advice and useful information, not otherwise easily procured, relating to the labourers and their families. In short, he does a great deal towards making it possible for gentlemen to exist upon their livings, with glebe and tithe in their present unsatisfactory condition. The farmer's wife is the best ally of the clergyman's wife. She helps in the village clothing-club, in the school and in the choir; and she, too, conveys a good deal of information to the parsonage, of which its inhabitants might have long remained in ignorance. That farmers of this class are able to help their own labourers in case of sickness or accident in a way which, to the man of fifty acres, would be impossible, "goes without saying." Finally, it may be added that the greater number of classes of which society consists, the greater its stability and steadiness, the greater room for the play of individual peculiarities, and the greater the security for the freedom and independence of minorities.

I don't think that any form of Dissent has ever prevailed very largely among the English farmers. In the old days, when the Church was to some extent unmindful of her pastoral duties, Dissent spread among the poor, because religion of some kind was necessary to them; and it is still. Those who go much among the London poor tell us that they cling to Christianity in some shape as the one great solace of their lot. And Methodism responded to a want which the Church at one time only very partially supplied. But it was scarcely felt by the farmers, with whom Dissent usually originated in a spirit of opposition, or a desire to spite somebody. If, according to our elegant euphemism, "any unpleasantness" arose between a farmer and his landlord on the question of tithes or rabbits, the former would take to going to chapel as the only way of paying him out. If the clergyman admonished him, or wounded the best feelings of his nature by thwarting him in the matter of pews —*belli teterrima causa* in country places—he did the same thing. But I doubt if he was often led thither by the wants of his spiritual nature. Once there, however, things were made very agreeable to him. He was caressed and flattered, and found himself a great man; and so the secession, which began in pique, was prolonged by vanity, and the Dissenters gained a new convert. But I should very much question whether he ever felt any preference for the chapel over the church on purely religious grounds.

I think, however, it must be admitted that where a farmer of the old school had any theological bias at all, it was slightly in favour of the Evangelical party. As a general rule, it did not occur to him to have any views at all upon such subjects. But he liked now and then a sensational sermon, as we like sensational novels; and the mysterious imagery of the Old Testament, combined with its intense human interest, had the same charm for him as it has for all people, I suppose, whose tastes have not been spoiled by education. Now the Evangelical clergy, in the days I am thinking of, were strong upon the Pentateuch; and I remember one who was very popular with village congregations because of his knowledge of "the types." An old man being reminded of him the other day, by a friend of the writer, showed what an impression every particular had made upon him. "Ah, sir," he said, "he wur oncommon good upon the types, specially the red heifer." Whether the fact of his living in a grazing country had caused this particular display of hermeneutic science to come home to him with peculiar force or not, I don't know. But that was the one thing that he remembered. There was, however, one religious feeling which burnt fiercely in the middle classes sixty years ago, and does still, and to which I have already referred. The British farmer, in common with the whole body of the English middle class, had always been brought up in intense horror of Romanism. The Roman Catholic Emancipation Act was not, as he knew, the fault of the English clergy. But they had been unable to prevent it; and *one* reason for his attachment to the National Church was gone. On the top of this rock of offence came the Tractarian movement, which woke his religious antipathies into new life, and wounded at the same time his religious conservatism. The levelling of the tall pews; the introduction of the surplice into the pulpit; the substitution of the harmonium or the organ for the fifes, flutes, trombones, and all kinds of music,[1] to which he had been accustomed from his childhood; the service on saints' days; the chanting, and the intoning,— were a severe shock to the farmer of sixty years of age, who had grown grey in the corner of his big pew, and whose dignity was hurt by being placed on a level with the common people. I

[1] These are being gradually restored.

have heard of such a man being taken suddenly ill, and obliged to leave the church, the first time he witnessed some of these startling innovations. Yet the great majority of them stood the strain very well, and remained faithful to the Church. And now a new generation has grown up familiar with the new system, and, I believe, partial to it. Yet still the feeling of the farmers towards the Church, however friendly, is not exactly what it was. They support the Church because they themselves like her services, and understand the advantages of an Establishment. But I doubt if they still look upon her with that kind of unquestioning veneration which animated their forefathers, when she was accepted as an inseparable part of the whole constitution of the country, the removal of which would be a moral and political convulsion too vast for their understandings to embrace.

The tithe question, which has revived again in our day, is quite a separate one. If the pinch of poverty has made the farmer impatient of legal obligation, and anxious to appropriate property which belongs to somebody else, it is from no aversion either to the Church or the clergy. He is desperate, and all due allowance must be made for the excesses of desperation. I should be afraid, however, that if the tithe question is kept open much longer, it may tend more and more to familiarise the farmer with the idea of disestablishment—not out of hostility to the Church, but from an idea that everybody should be allowed to give what he likes. The farmers, of course, really give nothing, and the whole share of the produce of the soil to which they are entitled, they still receive. Tithe is no more "a gift" to the Church than rent is to the landlord. I believe the majority of the farmers see the truth through all their vexation and confusion, and that all they want is a proportionate reduction of tithe. But there is certainly a minority who are gradually fanning themselves into a feeling of opposition to the principle, and who are heard to say that they would pay twice as much as their tithe to support the Church of England, if she waived her claim to it of right.

I have little to add to what I have already said

of the farmer's ideas about the land. He finds himself in a desperate predicament, and naturally looks round for somebody on whom he can throw the blame. He is hurt and angry, but is loath to be angry with himself. Like a wounded animal, he will turn upon his best friends. Here is no cause either for wonder or reproach. As he sees "his noble industry, the invention of gods and the occupation of heroes,"[1] rapidly giving way beneath his feet, we need not be surprised that he grows irritable, suspicious, and credulous; listens to the wildest nostrums, and clings vainly to the hope that, by some change of tenure or some legislative interference, the mischief which has been wrought by inevitable natural laws may be undone, and his old prosperity restored. Some still think a cure is to be found in increased security of tenure. But, waiving the question whether increased security of tenure could really do for the existing race of tenant-farmers what some of them imagine that it would, we have still to consider that there are many large

[1] Lord Beaconsfield.

landed proprietors who, sooner than part with all control over their own estates, or sink into the position of annuitants, would turn farmers themselves and solve the problem in that fashion. If the contention is true on which this demand is based—namely, that with increased security, farming could still be made profitable, even with rent to be paid—it is manifest that the landowner, who has no rent to pay, whose security is absolute, and who, in regard to capital, must, as a general rule, be in quite as favourable a position as the tenant-farmer, would be strongly tempted to try the experiment himself.

The landed proprietors of England are badly off just now, no doubt; but by their own showing the farmers are still worse off. What can *they* do with increased security of tenure, which their landlords could not do much better? Of course there is another way out of the situation, though it is not one which can be agreeable for the farmers to contemplate. If all that is wanted to restore the prosperity of English agriculture is a fair field for the safe investment of capital, the rich man may come in from the outside with more money than either landlord or tenant, and make terms with the owner which he might be only too glad to accept. Suppose the farms on any large estate to be taken up by an individual or a company as a purely commercial undertaking, many causes of friction which now exist between owner and occupier would be absent. Social jealousies, sporting jealousies, ecclesiastical difficulties would all disappear. The landlord would have whatever he chose to pay for, without any grumbling or ill-feeling. I, for one, have no desire at all to see such a change take place. I should deeply regret it. But it is one of the possibilities of the future on which the farmers would do well to ponder. If the old relations between landlord and tenant, between farmer and labourer, are all to be swept away—and I am told I am much too optimistic in expecting anything else—the consummation I have here indicated is not much more improbable than others which the landed interest has been taught to anticipate. It is a little so—because the man who was looking only to commercial results without any eye to the pleasures or the dignity of a landed proprietor, could find many more profitable investments for his money than agriculture. Still, it is one of those possibilities which have to be taken into account in considering the future of English farmers.

It will be observed that there is a broad line of demarcation to be drawn between the discontent of the farmer with the existing state of things and the discontent of the peasantry. The former is due almost exclusively to the bad times, very slightly flavoured on particular estates with some traditional soreness about game. But since the Act of 1880 this feeling has almost totally disappeared, and the English farmers are even calling out for some modification of the Act, in the shape of a close time for hares. Farmers are born sportsmen; and it requires only the exercise of a little courtesy and forbearance by the landlords to secure the absence of any trouble upon this score. The mainspring of the farmer's discontent is pecuniary. He has no social ambition or social jealousy to gratify. He would be only too happy to continue to be a farmer, and is pricked by no cravings after any higher kind of existence. The agricultural labourer is tired of being an agricultural labourer. He sighs for a different kind of life, with more excitement, more possibilities, more opportunities. The farmer's dissatisfaction springs chiefly from material causes; the labourer's from moral.

But there are certain general truths which may be predicted of both alike. Our political action is necessarily largely regulated by our material interests and our immediate wants, and the lower we descend in the social scale, the more absorbing do these wants and interests become, and the less do they admit of being modified by higher or more remote considerations. The most transient and superficial antagonism between these primary necessities, and measures based on any scientific or philosophic social principle which appears to clash with them, is sufficient to condemn the latter in the minds of uneducated men. It is difficult, therefore, to regard without anxiety the transfer of power from the more cultivated and enlightened to the more ignorant and illiterate classes which is now in progress in the English counties. The territorial aristocracy occupy a very different position from that of the commercial aristocracy. The only hostility which the latter have to fear from their work-people in the towns is based on economic grounds. No class is in arms against them but such as are at war with capital. A majority even of the Radical and Liberal party is on their side. But the landowners are assailed not only because they are monopolists, but because they are patricians. They are exposed to a converging fire from the enemies of wealth and the enemies of birth alike. Should the peasantry who have taken the Radical shilling show any signs of flagging, there is always a contingent at hand to egg them on to fresh efforts, or denounce them as degraded and spiritless. In other words, the aristocracy have to reckon with the organised forces of a powerful political party, as well as with the fitful and sporadic discontent of their own immediate dependants. It is, however, encouraging to perceive that some effort is to be made to retain the administration of the new system in the hands of the same class of men who so successfully administered the old one. The local aristocracy and the better class of farmers are everywhere coming forward to claim their proper place in the remodelled county constitution; and if their claims are recognised, as in the first instance they probably will be, much of the apprehended evil may be either averted, neutralised, or postponed.

The relations between the gentry and the farmers may not be all that could be wished; and I am assured that in some rural districts the farmers, as a rule, will assume a hostile attitude towards the magistrates under the new system which is now about to be inaugurated. I cannot speak with any certainty on this point myself; but I shall be surprised to learn that such feelings are at all general. I believe there are parts of the country where the farmers are under some vague impression that the country gentlemen might have done more for them, though goodness knows exactly what it is that they are thinking of. But I have no expectation that they will offer any organised opposition to the claims of the country gentlemen to take a principal part, as they have always done, in the management of county business, and to be looked up to by the rural population as their natural leaders. Other people may, but not the farmers. There will be isolated cases of antagonism, I have no doubt. There are rifts and flaws in the agricultural and territorial fabric, I am aware, which make me say that the relation between its component classes are not all that could be desired. But I believe that, on the whole, its main walls are still sound and solid, and that, for anything the farmers are likely to do, it may, with a few judicious repairs, weather many storms yet.

Much, no doubt, has passed away which will never return. The combined effects of agricultural depression and Radical agitation have worked a revolution in the course of twenty years which, under ordinary circumstances, it might have taken near a century to effect. But quite enough of the old system still remains to make it worth while to keep up the struggle in support of it.

THE PEASANTRY.

"Oft did the harvest to their sickle yield,
   Their furrow oft the stubborn glebe has broke:
How jocund did they drive their team afield!
   How bowed the woods beneath their sturdy stroke!"

I HAVE often thought that in these lines we have represented to us the three most characteristic and picturesque operations of rural industry—ploughing the ground, reaping the harvest, and felling the timber in the brown autumn woodlands. Throwing ourselves for a moment into the spirit of the poet, we see the sturdy English peasant going forth to his work in the fresh early morning, well clothed, well fed, cheerful and contented: out at the farmyard gates, past the rugged elms and the ivy-mantled tower, across the brook, and up to the accustomed hill, there to labour steadily till the declining sun warns him to unyoke his weary horses and bring them back with loosened traces to the old moss-grown stable. We watch him shouldering his sickle under the bright and dewy August sunrise, and speeding over the dank greensward for a long day among the yellow corn till the moon is high in heaven. Or we follow him to the November woods, ankle-deep in dead leaves, surrounded by fallen trunks—a scene that Linnell loved—and wielding his axe with right good will against the oak, the ash, or the beech, till the waning light warns him to plod home again to his cottage on the edge of the common, with its garden and its orchard, its pigsty, its cowshed, and its henroost, to eat his bacon and potatoes by the fireside, and hear the village news till it is time for him to tumble into bed, tired, happy, with a good conscience, and without a care.

Such is the picture which it requires no effort of the imagination to conjure up before us as we read these well-known stanzas, written some hundred and forty years ago—for we are entitled to believe that they represent only the actual truth. They recall to us a time when, according to Mr Hallam, the tillers of the soil in England lived in great comfort, when the "happy peasant" pursued the even tenor of his way, with enough for all his humble wants, and asking no more; catching only at intervals faint murmurs from the outside world through the waggoner or the post-boy; with elbow-room for himself and his children, and the prospect of a decent support in his old age, without misery or disgrace; when the whole country life of England basked in a kind of afternoon repose, and rural felicity was not entirely a dream.

Why should it be so now? and is it, indeed, really so? No doubt, between the end of the reign of George II. and the close of the American war there is a great gulf fixed. During this interval prices rose without any corresponding rise in wages: and although too great stress may have been laid on the numerous Enclosure Acts which were passed in the early part of George III.'s reign—since the more land that was brought under tillage, the more employment there would be—still the fact remains that these Acts did deprive the peasantry of the commons, and swallow up at the same time various little bits of waste ground which they had made their own. The French war found them with crippled resources, ill prepared to face the new troubles that awaited them. Mr Pitt had a scheme for their relief, which, like all his schemes, was bold and comprehensive, but which would rather hurt the feelings of modern ratepayers and shock the prejudices of modern political economists. He proposed that industrial schools should be established in all the villages of the kingdom, and that the parish officer should be empowered to levy the necessary rates; and, what is more to the present purpose, that any person entitled to receive parish relief might take a lump sum in advance to enable him or her to buy a cow or a pig, or pay the rent of a small plot of ground.

The pressure of foreign affairs prevented Pitt from proceeding any further with his scheme; and instead of it, an Act was passed in 1795 empowering the parish authorities to give relief in aid of wages to able-bodied men. The remedy was worse than the disease; and matters became so intolerable in the course of forty years, that the new poor-law, rushing into the opposite extreme, was the natural result. Many people thought that, instead of breaking up the old parochial system, it would have been quite sufficient to repeal the Act of 1795, before which time no complaints had been made, either of the mode in which the law was administered, or the influence which it exercised on the people. Of the bitter hatred with which the new system was regarded by the agricultural poor for many years after its first introduction, I retain a lively recollection. I remember, as a child, being puzzled at hearing the workhouse called the "bastyle" by the village labourers, with a strong emphasis on the second syllable; and I have always believed that it was the first thing which disturbed to any serious extent the old feelings of amity and loyalty between the peasantry and the gentry.

The old system was marked by grave abuses. But it was not one, as Mr Canning used to say, to be abolished with a light heart; and he attributed the peace and prosperity of England and the loyalty of the people during many very trying periods mainly to the existence of the old poor-law, which gave them a hold upon the land and attached them to the gentry, who were really relieving them out of their own pockets. I am not aware that the peasantry in those days were a peculiarly abject race, or deficient in independence and self-respect. Before the Act of 1795 they certainly would have contrasted very favourably in this respect with the labourers of to-day. This Act had the very opposite effect to that which was expected from it. An old labourer in Gloucestershire told one of the Commissioners in 1834 that he had often heard his father-in-law say, " What a sad change there was now going on in the parish! and that he remembered the time when a man would rather starve than apply: but that nowadays a man was more employed because he went on the parish, than because he was industrious and tried to keep off."

It seems reasonable to believe, therefore, that the Act of 1834 went beyond the necessities of the case. Under the old system outdoor relief was granted on a magistrate's order, and this created a close and intimate connection between the landed proprietors and the poor, which had existed for centuries, and which it should have been the first object of Conservative statesmen to defend. Men's minds, however, were in no mood for moderate measures, and a blow was then struck at our old rural constitution, from which it has never entirely recovered.

During the whole of this time, and for some years afterwards, the agricultural interest, in spite of the corn laws, was very much depressed, and the labourers were very badly off. Rick-burning and machine-burning became common: and it was not until the social and monetary system of the country —deranged, firstly, by the long war, and secondly, by the peace which put an end to it—gradually righted itself, that the murmurs of agrarian discontent began to die away, or were lost in the louder wail of of the factory operative.

From about the year 1840 down to the great agricultural strike of 1870, the world heard little of the agricultural labourer. The interest of the philanthropical public now became concentrated on the artisan class, on the truck system, and on factory tyranny. But after these grievances had been redressed and political rights conferred upon town populations by the bill of 1867, the public had leisure to turn once more to the condition of the peasantry. Although this was still far from satisfactory, it was evident that during the last thirty years their position had been steadily improving. In some of the English counties, the south-western counties especially, they had made perhaps but little progress. Elsewhere, it may be doubted whether they had not so far regained the ground lost during the dreary interval I have mentioned—that is, from about 1815 to 1840—as to reinvest the old-fashioned conception of rustic happiness with some tints of its original reality. In the year 1847, Mr Frederick Clifford visited East Anglia as correspondent for the 'Times' newspaper, just when the quarrel between farmers and labourers was at its height. His letters were published afterwards in a volume styled the 'Agricultural Look-out'; and in the tenth chapter of that book will be found a description of the peasantry which strongly confirms the supposition. The peasantry of the eastern counties were not exceptionally well off. And what was true of them then, is still more true of them now. But Mr Clifford concludes this chapter with the following words:—

"A few visits paid by intelligent working men in towns to an average country village would do them more good than joining a mob of holiday excursionists to the seaside, and would probably dispel some illusions about rural serfs and their brutal oppressors. I doubt also whether the sight of pretty roomy cottages, gardens gay with flowers, well-cropped allotments, leafy lanes, and green fields, would not send a good many back to town regretting that their lines had not fallen in such pleasant places, or, at all events, feeling that rural life, if the reward of labour be small, has many and great compensations."

These words were written fourteen years ago; and now that a new future seems to be opening before the agricultural labourer, it may be well perhaps to take another glance at his progress, and learn what we can of his material welfare, his character, and his aspirations at this particular moment. The late Mr Jefferies has given us in 'Hodge and his Masters' a fairly complete account of the peasantry of the southern counties. But that was written nearly ten years ago, and events have moved rapidly in the interval. There are, too, some phases of English rural life which did not come quite within the range of his vision; or, at all events, which he did not understand so well as others: and I doubt whether any one, anxious to foretell the future of the English counties, would be justified in relying exclusively on the data supplied by this ingenious and picturesque writer.

The first thing to be done is to obtain a general, but as far as possible an exact, view of the physical and economical condition of the labourer at this present moment. That must be the basis of all further inquiries. When we know that, we have firm ground to stand upon, and can pursue our speculations on his moral and intellectual characteristics in comparative security. With regard to his material condition, something like certainty is attainable: and I must protest at the outset against that method of criticism which proceeds on the assumption that all statements of this nature are more or less ingenious guesses, and that none of them are based on actually ascertained facts. In the very brief survey of the labourer's material position, which is all that it will be necessary to lay before the reader in this chapter, all conclusions not deduced from official sources are derived partly from personal experience, partly from answers to questions addressed directly by myself to residents in the country, and in some instances to those who have worked as day-labourers themselves.[1]

The latest official information on the whole subject is to be found in the evidence taken before the Duke of Richmond's Commission, 1879-1882, and the reports thereunto annexed. Another very useful work is 'The History and Present Condition of the Allotment System' (1886), by the Earl of Onslow. And the information contained in them I have myself supplemented, as already stated, by direct personal inquiries in the spring of 1887.[2] One cannot stereotype the condition of any class: wages and prices may differ a little to-day from what they were fifteen months ago:

[1] See 'The Agricultural Labourer.' By T. E. Kebbel. Allen & Co. 1887. [2] Ibid.

but no such depression or deviation has occurred on either side as to throw my account off its balance and necessitate a fresh adjustment.

The title of the work of Mr Jefferies to which I have just referred is, it may be observed, 'Hodge *and* his Masters'; that is to say, it is a book about farmers and landlords as well as about Hodge himself—in other words, about all three branches of the agricultural interest. And he says himself in his preface, "The labourer at the present moment has the best of the bargain." I am anxious to call particular attention to this point, because one of my main objects will be to show that, in calculating the line of conduct likely to be adopted by the peasantry under the new responsibilities thrown upon them — in striving to get behind mere appearances, and to penetrate to their inner motives,[1]—we must allow no place in our account for exceptional physical distress, or for any sense of injustice provoked by a comparison of their present lot with anything they have enjoyed within

[1] As the 'Spectator,' in some comments on the above-mentioned work of mine, invited me to do.

the reach of rural memories or traditions. I must ask my readers, therefore, to start with me (under protest if they please) from this position—namely, that the English peasantry are in all material respects better off now than they have been at any time during the last hundred and twenty years—and this not only absolutely but relatively,—better off in proportion to the prosperity of the other agricultural classes.

A very few pages will be sufficient to show what grounds we have for arriving at this conclusion. But before entering upon particulars it may not be unnecessary even now to caution the reader once more against the common error of confounding wages with income, and of supposing that when the labourer has received his allotted number of shillings on Saturday night he has nothing more to depend on. His wages on an average do not represent more than three-quarters of his income.

Wages,[1] perquisites, and agricultural customs

---

[1] By wages are meant the weekly money which the labourer receives every Saturday night. By perquisites are meant: 1. The

differ so greatly in various parts of England, that a resident in the north, acquainted only with the system prevailing in his own country, would very likely be inclined at first sight to dispute the accuracy of figures relating to the south and south-west. But it appears, on the whole, that the total yearly income of an ordinary English day-labourer, including both wages and perquisites of every kind, ranges from about £50 a-year in Northumberland to a little over £30 in Wiltshire and other south-western counties. This gives an average of £40 a-year.[1] But it is only the exceptionally low wages paid in a few counties which pulls down the average even so low as this. In the eastern, midland, northern, and south-east counties it is commoner to find the sum-total rising to £43 and £44 than sinking to £37 or £38. Shepherds, waggoners, and stockmen are

difference between the rent which he pays for his cottage, and the rent which it is really worth; 2. Harvest-money; 3. Beer; 4. Fagots; 5. Driving coals; 6. Bacon; 7. Potatoes; and there may be more, according to the different customs of different counties.

[1] *I.e.*, Average wages 12s. a-week; value of perquisites about 4s. a-week.

paid at a higher rate, and their wages average about £50 a-year.[1]

Before the Education Act of 1870 came into general operation,[2] and when it was more usual for women to work in the fields than it is now, the earnings of the labourer's wife and family made a considerable addition to his yearly income. Where women are employed now, they earn from 4s. to 6s. a-week at ordinary times, and from 10s. to 12s. in harvest. From juvenile labour, as boys can usually get to work by the time they are twelve or thirteen, I calculate the average addition to the cottage income to be about £18 a-year. Throw in an average of £2 a-year for the women, which is certainly much below the mark, and that gives a total average of £60 as the annual income

---

[1] Our authorities for these figures have been given on the foregoing page. They are the Report of the Duke of Richmond's Commission, 1879-1882, especially Mr Druce's Table of Wages; a paper in the 'Royal Agricultural Society's Journal,' by Mr Little, 1878; and thirty returns obtained by the present writer from farmers and landowners in twenty-seven representative counties in 1887.

[2] The Commissioners in 1867 calculated that the withdrawal from farm-work of children under ten years of age would involve an average loss to the parents of £4 or £5 a-year.

of an able-bodied English peasant, where he has the help of wife and children.

Under the head of perquisites, I include cottages and gardens, let to the labourer considerably below their real value. But I have not included the value of his garden-produce, nor yet whatever profit he may make from his allotment, both of which must therefore be added to the above total. The net profit on an allotment of one rood is usually calculated at about £5 a-year.

Such being his income, we have next to consider what he can buy with it; and this much seems to be certain at any rate, that he can buy more with it now than he could have done at almost any time within the present century. Ordinary commodities—bread, mutton, bacon, cheese, butter, tea and sugar, boots, shoes, and coats—are all from 20 to 30 per cent cheaper than they were eighteen years ago, while wages are just about the same. The village labourer now is a wholly different man from what he was in the last generation. He wears different clothes, eats different food, lives in a different house, and works in a different manner. He wears broadcloth on Sundays, and sometimes at his work too. The old smock-frock is entirely discarded, except by a few village patriarchs, who cling to it just as gentlemen here and there clung to their pigtails in the reign of George IV. That decent garb will soon become a thing of the past, equally with the more picturesque velveteen coat, corduroy knee-breeches, well-fitting grey worsted stockings, and neat well-greased boots, which formed the Sunday attire of the younger peasantry thirty years ago. They must all now have their black coats to their backs, and badly made trousers on their legs, and badly polished boots on their feet; the consequence being that they do not look a quarter so much like gentlemen as they did in their old costume; and are all the poorer for looking all the more vulgar.

The average day-labourer in regular work now eats butcher's meat much oftener than he used to do. He will often have broiled ham for breakfast; and at harvest-time, when his wife, or oftener his little girl, carries out "father's tea" to him in the meadows, if you lift the corner of her apron, or peep into her basket, ten to one you will find a tin of preserved salmon or a box of sardines stowed away between the loaf and the jug. Look into the window of the village shop and see the tale it tells,—tinned meats and soups, delicacies and "kickshaws," which, to "the rude forefathers of the hamlet," would have seemed as strange and wonderful as the Tokay and Johannisberg of Lord de Mowbray seemed to the savages of Hell House Yard. Grocery and chandlery are now brought round to the villages in vans at a much lower rate than the local shopkeepers can afford to sell them at. Necessaries are far cheaper than they were in the labourer's childhood, and luxuries have now become as cheap as necessaries were then.

I would avoid wearying the reader with statistics while still on the threshold of the subject. I will only add, therefore, that the labourers' cottages, as a rule, are far better than they used to be; that landowners have almost everywhere been making great efforts to provide proper accommodation for the peasantry on their own estates; and that the decrease of the village population has in many places caused the supply of cottages to be in excess of the demand. The hovels which still exist under the name of cottages almost always belong either to the occupiers themselves, who sturdily refuse to quit them, or else to speculative builders in some adjoining town, who have run them up as cheaply, and charge for them as dearly, as they can. The labourer may still be dissatisfied with his lodging, but he knows perfectly well that it is a great advance on what it used to be, that it is improving every day, and that if it is not better, it is not the fault of the Squire.

Next we come to the allotment system — and on this subject great misapprehensions prevailed down to the passing of Lord Onslow's Act, when, however, public interest being aroused, the question was examined and many foolish errors put to rout. A little while before the passing of this bill, Lord Onslow himself had written a book upon allotments, the contents of which were abundantly confirmed by the parliamentary debates which followed. All that those who had been loudest in their denunciations of the landowners now found to say was that, although the demand for allotments had been all but entirely supplied by voluntary effort, still it was desirable to have an Act of Parliament to provide for the very few instances in which it had not. Besides Lord Onslow's book, we have the Government returns published last year; and it is now known, or easily may be known, to all who will take the trouble to inquire, that of the whole number of agricultural labourers in England and Wales only a very small percentage are without either allotments, cottage-gardens, or cow-runs. According to the census returns of 1881, the number of *bonâ fide* agricultural labourers in England and Wales was 807,608. We know that they have not increased in number since that time; and according to official statements in 1887, the number of allotments, gardens, and cow-runs amounted to 654,028, of these 389,000 being allotments.

But what it is also very interesting to know is this: that, according to the evidence collected by Lord Onslow, and published only two years ago, in many English counties allotments were at that date going begging. The old tenants had voluntarily abandoned them, and no new ones could be found to take their places. It was not the rent that was deterrent; for in some cases this was lower than the agricultural rent of the district, in many it was just the same, and in only a few a little higher. Nor can the fact be entirely owing to the distance of the allotments from the villages; for I can remember allotment-grounds more than half a mile from the nearest cottage for which there was a regular scramble as soon as a vacancy occurred, though now it appears half of them are on the landlords' hands. Whether this has anything to do with the development of a new trait in the agricultural labourer—the dislike, namely, of hard work—may be worth consideration. Of allotments I will conclude by saying that, though the system is sometimes spoken of by self-constituted champions of the peasantry as if it was a new thing, it has been in existence since the beginning of the century, and was taken up generally by the country clergy, who were the first to appreciate its benefits, at least sixty years ago.

It will now be seen, I think, that if the English peasantry have any reason to be dissatisfied with their present lot, it can hardly be on the ground of physical privations. We are none of us so well off but what we might be better; and unquestionably the agricultural labourer may legitimately aspire to a somewhat higher life than he leads at present. But he is better off relatively than either the proprietor or the tenant-farmer. They have sunk in the scale of prosperity; he has risen. He enjoys comforts and luxuries unknown to his fathers and grandfathers; while they have been obliged to abandon what their fathers and grandfathers enjoyed. He is not obliged to work so hard as he did formerly, nor to begin work so young; and he is educated a great deal better. Where then does the shoe pinch, if it does pinch? Why are the peasants leaving the land, as we are told they are, and crowding into the large towns? Why is skilled agricultural labour growing scarcer and scarcer in our villages, and why are the farmers complaining that they cannot get their ground properly cultivated owing to the fact that the labourers who remain behind are too stupid, too indolent, or too indifferent to learn the details of agriculture? To know this, one might almost say, would be to know everything—to know what is passing in the minds of the most active and intelligent of the peasantry as well as in the minds of the most sluggish, and to be able to give a good guess at what they are likely to do with the power newly placed in their hands. Of the facts themselves, I am afraid there can be no doubt. The exodus of the peasantry is a fact. The inferiority for all agricultural purposes of those who stay at home is a fact. The Richmond Commission is a witness to this. But what would keep the better ones at home, or stimulate the worse to greater exertions and to a more lively interest in the work they are called on to perform, are questions not so easily answered.

I am allowing the hypothesis on which the whole discussion hangs—namely, that discontent *does* exist among the English peasantry to a perceptible if not to a serious extent—to pass unchallenged. We had better see it where it does not exist, than not see it where it does. Besides, though I think it is much exaggerated, I do not think it wholly imaginary. It is no very difficult thing in this world, of course, to set class against class; and in some parts of England, I daresay the labourers may have been taught to think that whatever they have to complain of in their lot is the doing of those above them, either the farmers or the gentry, or both. It is a very exceptional state of things indeed in which there will not be from time to time some kind of friction in the relations between employers and employed. No doubt the labourers in many counties at this moment are grumbling at their wages and girding at the farmers. But they understand something about farming. They can calculate pretty well what wages the farmer can afford to pay, and what rent the landlord is entitled to demand; and I see no evidence that there is among them any widespread or deeply rooted feeling that they are being treated with injustice. What they do think, I believe, is, that if the farmers cannot cultivate the land themselves, they might as well give the labourers a chance. Anything, they think, would be better than letting it remain as it is. On a certain percentage of the peasantry we may suppose that this view of the land question does operate with more or less effect. But my own opinion is, that we must go behind this if we want to get at the root of the matter. Different motives springing from distinct sources may converge towards similar results in the long-run; and it may very well be that the vague kind of dissatisfaction which prompts the labourer to leave his home, may ultimately be allayed by some readjustment of the land question. But the land question is only very partially the cause of it at the present moment.

Assuming, then, that dissatisfaction to a greater or less degree does exist, let us take one by one the various reasons which have been given for it, and the various remedies which have been suggested. Some say that what the emigrants want is "a better position" generally, than they occupy as farm-labourers, even at the best; and that as they cannot get it on the land they go to seek it in the town. Others say that they have acquired a taste for the excitement and the pleasures of a town life, and that nothing now would retain them in a country village. If so, it is a bad look-out for English agriculture. Sometimes we are told that they wish to become farmers, or to see a fair prospect of becoming farmers, on their own account, by the time they have passed middle age; that they are tired of being dependent all their lives, and wish to have something to fight for, as the artisan has — the chance, that is, of becoming a master man. A fourth class say that they cannot stand the cottages; and a fifth, that they go away simply because they cannot get work, while all the time the farmers say they cannot get labour. Sixthly, it is urged that the peasantry leave the land because there is no longer enough under the plough to find employment for them, and likewise that machinery has lessened the demand for agricultural hands.

I will not say but what there may be an element of truth in all and each of the above theories. Those who converse with the educated young labourer of the present day, will perceive that he is thinking of things only indirectly connected with the conditions of agriculture. With his former garb he has cast his former self.[1] He has lost his relish for the country. He will tell you, if you can only lead him on to talk frankly, that village life is "a poor thing": that is a favourite phrase with him. He will declare that his native village is "a poor place"—and that not from any fancied sense of personal superiority in himself, but really because it fails to satisfy those newly felt yearnings in his own heart which education has planted there. He is conscious that an agricultural labourer is not so important a member of society as an artisan. He has no corporate life: no institute, no discussion, no power. The artisan seems to breathe a larger and freer moral and intellectual atmosphere. The young labourer has read quite enough at the board school to put thoughts of this kind into his head. Tennyson, referring to a different class of society, has described the feelings of a country-bred youth on first seeing

---

[1] These remarks refer only to one class of the peasantry—those who are on the move—not to those who still cultivate the soil.

the lights of London, in words which express very much my own meaning :—

> "And his spirit leaps within him to be gone before him, then,
> Underneath the light he looks at, in among the throngs of men."

Something of this kind of longing has now, I think, penetrated down to the agricultural labourer. The young, clever, well-educated peasant wants to be something more than the best ploughman or the best thatcher in the village. It is not with him a question of wages. Young, unmarried, skilful, and intelligent, if he gives his mind to farmwork, he may earn wages that will give him all he wants and more. It is not altogether a question of the land either. He knows what kind of life the owner of three or four acres leads, and it has few charms for him compared with pushing his fortune in the city.

Town life to the labourer seems fraught with indefinite possibilities to which the country affords no parallel; and since his imagination has once been stirred by them, he will never again be exactly what he was before. Setting aside, however, all these glittering visions, the practical common-sense view of the matter is, that he sees in the town opportunities of rising in life which do not exist in the country. They do not exist for the farmer, nor yet for the squire, any more than they do for the labourer. Their place in society is fixed. But the peasant sees that artisans become shopkeepers, that shopkeepers become merchants, and that merchants become merchant princes. If such thoughts ever entered into his head in the old days, they remained thoughts only. He did not know how to go to work to begin a new career. But schools and railways have taught him; and in less than another generation the peasant of the olden time — the peasant of Gray's Elegy, the peasant of George Eliot, contented to end his days as he began them in his native village, satisfied with his own position, and without a wish to rise out of that station in life to which it had pleased God to call him—will probably be quite extinct.

That the pleasures and the excitement of a town life, quite apart from the opening which it affords to the more enterprising and aspiring spirits, tend to draw the labourer away from home, is only natural and probable; and there is this not unimportant fact to be remembered, that when the labourer calls his village life "a poor thing," it really is a poor thing in one sense compared with what it used to be within living memory. It may be that the younger labourers, if they could suddenly be thrown back for a generation, retaining at the same time their present tastes and habits, would not care for the pleasures which satisfied their grandfathers.

"The sports of children satisfy the child;"

and the labourer has put away childish things. But there is no doubt that the life of an English village at the present day is duller than it was fifty years ago. Different customs prevailed in different parts of England; but everywhere the villages kept up old festivals and traditional rejoicings with a heartiness which has now died out. I cannot remember the May-pole, and have only seen a limited number of village greens of the old-fashioned cut; but the "feast" or "wake," which is still not entirely extinct, was in many English counties thirty years ago a kind of village carnival, to which the whole population looked forward with intense delight. Most of the cottagers had then their friends and relatives to stay with them, and the poorest had a large piece of beef, a plum-pudding, and a bottle of home-made wine. The children who were out at service always came home for the feast—or fee-ast, as it was pronounced in the midland counties; and by some of the more privileged among the matrons the parson's children would be asked to tea. The village street in the evening, if the feast came in the summer was a regular promenade. Booths and caravans, with all kinds of shows, toys, and sweets, stood on each side; and, as I need not say, the public-houses drove a roaring trade. The principal farmers did not in those days think it *infra dig.* to follow the example of the labourers; and they, too, used generally to have their houses full at the feast. It was a great time, too, for weddings; and also for fights. The champions of two neighbouring villages would often make a match to come off at the feast, besides the numerous scratch encounters got up over the pipes and ale. The feast began on the saint's day to whom the church was dedicated, or the Sunday nearest to it, and usually lasted a week. It afforded matter to talk of for three months before it began and for three months after it was over.

I have known villages elsewhere where the great festival was on Trinity Sunday, and on the Monday evening the whole village danced upon the parson's lawn. Then there were Christmas-day, and Plough Monday, and Whitsuntide, and other time-honoured occasions which brought their appropriate diversions, but which now, from all I can ascertain, if still observed, have lost much of their former light-hearted joviality. Above all, there was the harvest-home, for which the modern harvest festival is no exact equivalent, though it may be, and no doubt is in some respects, a great improvement on it. But there is not the freedom, the licence, and the old joviality of the farmhouse kitchen in these modern entertainments. They are not "cakes and ale," and can never be equally attractive to the younger generation, who will have their fling in one way or another, let the moralists say what they please.

In the days of old, then, the village was a little self-contained community, with its own simple round of amusements and interests, providing sufficient excitement for a population which knew no others, and rearing generation after generation of sturdy agricultural labourers, who accepted their vocation as a law of nature, and never looked beyond it. Village life was not dull to *them*, partly because it really was more cheerful and diversified in itself than it is at present, partly because the labourer had not learned to look abroad and compare Mantua with Rome.

Nearly all the young men in the rural districts between the ages of eighteen and twenty-five have now passed through the educational process. It has opened a new world to them. Who ever could have expected it to be otherwise? It has thoroughly unsettled them, and till the process of fermentation is over we must be prepared for startling phenomena. The danger is lest what is only the natural disturbance consequent on a period of transition, should be mistaken for the symptoms of deep and permanent disaffection with the structure and conditions of society. One cure for this form of discontent, the first upon our list, is the district or the parish council. When the peasant finds he can be "as big a man" in his native village as in the adjoining town, his principal inducement to leave the country will, it is thought, disappear.

But if what we have here said has any element of truth in it, such will not be the effect. The parish council would not make him as big a man as he imagines he can make himself by migrating to the town. It will not materially alter his position in life. Farmer or labourer, he would be a peasant still. Much is written and spoken of the stimulating effect of corporate or municipal life. It is forgotten that in large towns there are always questions arising to keep that life in activity. But in an ordinary-sized village this would be impossible; and either the institution would stagnate and wither, or fall into the hands of wire-pullers and busybodies, who would speedily disgust all the respectable inhabitants, whether farmers, labourers, or gentlemen, with the whole concern. There is no magic in names or in forms of government. To force local institutions into being where there is really nothing for them to live upon, so far from creating that spirit in the people which it is thought desirable to arouse, will only have the opposite effect of bringing the institution itself into contempt.

The Report of the Poor Law Commissioners in 1834, pages 107-118, on Parish Vestries, will be found to throw a good deal of light on the question of parish councils.

When Mr Morley recently sketched out the functions which, in his opinion, should be intrusted to parish councils, what kind of parishes could possibly have been present to his mind? Does he seriously suppose that in an English agricultural village, with a population of two hundred people, there are to be found the materials for a representative assembly competent to deal with such questions as charities, allotments, public buildings, common lands, and compulsory acquisition of land for public purposes; or that, even if there were, anything could be found for them to do? In the vast majority of English villages the allotment system is already established; and where it is not, could only be established once. The public buildings in many such places are limited to the parish pound, and the old rotten stocks still standing in the neighbourhood of the public-house. In a great many there are neither charities nor common lands. And in very few are the charities of sufficient importance to afford any employment to a parish council. Is a council composed of such materials to have the power of levying rates, and of deciding what portions of the land belonging to their neighbours is to be appropriated to their own use? We can scarcely believe that Mr Morley meant this. Yet such is the impression which his language leaves upon the reader.

Whether the newly awakened ambition of the peasantry, and their desire to find themselves in a position where, in common with their fellow-labourers in the town, they may have opportunities of rising, will be satisfied by providing them with greater facilities for obtaining land of their own, is a question which it is useless either to ask or to answer till we can make up our minds on the possibility of establishing in this country the system of petty culture on a large scale, and as an important and substantial branch of our agricultural economy. The exceptionally industrious, skilful, and economical labourer never had any difficulty in obtaining "a bit of land" for himself by the time he was forty or fifty years of age; and has less now than ever. But, as I have already stated, I doubt if the class of men who are now turning to the towns would care to live as he does, always supposing them to be possessed of the same qualifications. The time may come when they will find out their mistake, and be glad to come back again to the land. But that time has not come yet. Meanwhile the provision of small farms for the peasantry indiscriminately would never work. At what age are they to have them, and on what conditions? The feeling of independence would reconcile them to hard living. To tell the ordinary peasant that as a small farmer he would have to work harder, live harder, and die sooner than the ordinary day-labourer, makes no impression on him;

his answer is that he would "chance that." He would readily pay that price to be his own master. But could the average English labourer live at all on a farm of four acres? not live well, but keep body and soul together? And would not the first pinch of adversity, or two or three bad seasons in succession, make an end of him? I think the more intelligent class of labourers would have but one answer to this question, and that it is this which sends them into the towns.

There is at present a self-acting principle of selection at work which will always provide for the best; but when we come down to the average, what is to be done then? On what principles are the candidates for public assistance to be chosen when one is as good as another? Will not an amount of jealousy and discontent be created by such a system, out of all proportion to the good done? Furthermore, it is said that such a measure will restore to the farmer the supply of labour which he wants. But the conversion of labourers into farmers does not seem a very promising method of producing that result either. The agricultural labourer will not consent to wait till he is an old man before he gets a farm. He will desire to obtain one when he is in the prime of life, and then what becomes of his usefulness to the farmer? Just as his skill and experience are becoming of the highest value to his employer, he will want to leave him.

Those labourers who are driven from the country simply because they cannot get work, have in most instances only themselves to blame. They can't *do* the work, and they won't learn it. This is the unanimous[1] testimony of farmers from all parts of England, north, south, east, and west. Formerly, when the better class of young men which produced the skilled labourer — the thatcher, the hedger, and the drainer — remained at home, they kept up the standard of work. Now that they are gone, it has fallen to a lower level. The labourers are listless and indifferent. Some kinds of farm-work they can't do at all, and what they can do they do badly. Few of them are fit to

---

[1] Duke of Richmond's Report (1879-81), *passim*. 'The Agricultural Labourer,' pp. 57-66.

be trusted with horses, or dumb animals in general. Many of them are men who have made a venture in the towns, but having neither the energy nor the talent to secure success, have wandered back to their native villages, rejected by the warehouse and spoiled for the corn-field. This is the material on which the farmers now have to work; and we can understand them saying that they cannot afford to pay such men high wages, and that they do not choose to make work for them when none is absolutely wanted.

With regard to the effect of machinery on the demand for agricultural labour, opinions seem to differ. Some say that it has had no effect at all; and even where it has, seeing that it is the best men who are in demand for the management of engines, the introduction of machinery can scarcely account for the migration of the best men.

No doubt the withdrawal of land from cultivation has injured the labourer's position; but the effect of it has been greatly overrated. If we take the number of acres of arable land which have gone out of cultivation during the agricultural depression, and then calculate the number of labourers which would ordinarily have been employed upon them, the product will account for only a small percentage of the emigrants.

We have now gone over the various causes to which the so-called "exodus" of the agricultural population may be attributed, and we find, as might be expected, that those who remain behind are inferior both in character and intelligence to those who have departed. We are next confronted with the fact that it will be these men, and not the peasantry of an earlier and better day, who will represent the peasant vote in the new scheme of county government. I for one should have no fear of that class of labourers from whom formerly came all the skilled workmen, and among whom every farmer found his right-hand man. These men, with their higher education and sharpened wits, have not parted with their old traditions and old associations, to fall under the yoke of new masters and become the cat's-paws of a selfish conspiracy. Supposing them to retain not a remnant of their former respect for the ancient proprietors of the soil, and the families with whom their ancestors have been connected for so many generations, they have got some ideas of political economy instead; while their minds have been sufficiently trained to accustom them to look a little way ahead in judging of questions which touch their own immediate interests. They would not be so likely as the more ignorant class whom they have left behind them, to judge of the small-farm question by its immediate benefits without looking to its ultimate results. Their minds would be capable of embracing both sides of the controversy; while on questions of pauperism and poor-relief, their own self-respect would be some guarantee against their sanctioning extreme courses.

But can we say as much of the residuum, left to their own sweet wills, and uncontrolled and uninfluenced by the more intelligent members of their order who have left the soil? I doubt it. It is among these, if anywhere among the peasantry, that the worst kind of demagogues will find their readiest tools and most ignorant and credulous disciples. It is among these that communistic doctrines may possibly make some progress — and any theories whatever which promise a day's independence, regardless of all future consequences. It is difficult to say exactly what thoughts are passing through their brains at this moment. Some of these men may fancy themselves ill-used; some few may cherish a grudge against the farmers; and a still smaller number may have been taught to see their enemies in the gentry. I fancy, however, that their feeling towards both is one rather of indifference. But they think a good deal of the "turn and turn about" doctrine. They have a kind of vague idea that it ought to be their turn now. The gentry and the farmers have had a good time of it, they think, for many centuries. Why should not they themselves have a slice of good fortune at last? I don't think they go further than this. Such ideas as that the land belongs to them; that they have been robbed of it; that the present owners are tyrants and oppressors,—I do not think have made much way with them. They apply the parable of Dives and

Lazarus to the conditions of this world. They think that those above them have had their good things, and likewise themselves evil things. They are therefore entitled to compensation. They have no dislike of gentlemen as such; nor do they want to be gentlemen themselves. They know very well that they have experienced nothing but kindness from the old families and from the clergy; and they have, as a rule, no angry feelings towards them. They have no desire to injure them for the sake of injuring them. They wish only to better themselves.

Their political creed was, and in many places still is, summed up in a very simple formula. There are two parties in the country—"the high party and the low party," whereof the latter, though it might naturally be supposed more in harmony with the lower orders, had, before he obtained the franchise, small hold upon the labourer's sympathies. In his inability to exercise any real political power, the labourer's politics ran in a traditional, and what might perhaps be called an emotional, channel. The old dislike and suspicion of Dissent, for instance, handed down from the seventeenth century, survived in great strength in the English rural districts less than twenty years ago; and the low party maintained equivocal relations with "Methodies," Ranters, Jumpers, *et hoc genus omne*, for whom the unsophisticated English peasant, with his innate sense of humour, entertained feelings the reverse of respectful. Then, again, the low party were supposed to be "agen the gentry"; and as there was nothing at that time to be gained by attacking these last, there was nothing to interrupt the free play of the labourer's natural inclinations, which were in favour of gentlemen as a class, though they might dislike particular individuals. Since they have obtained the franchise, however, they have come to see the low party in rather a different light; and the conflict between their ancient prepossessions and their material interests, as these are represented to them by the "low" connection, is now very perceptible, and is, in fact, the most important factor in the political situation of the day. As I have already stated, I don't think their feelings towards the clergy and gentry are less friendly than they were, except in so far as they present any obstacles to the realisation of those golden dreams in which the rural demagogue has taught them to believe. But as far as he *has* taught them to believe in these, he has doubtless arrayed them to some extent against the owners and occupiers of the soil.[1] It is the old story. And how long the delusion will last it is impossible to say. The peasantry, however, are in course of being educated. They nourish no resentment against " nouns and verbs and such abominations," so it may be hoped they will find out the truth before irreparable harm is done.

[1] Speaking of these same golden dreams and reckless promises, a statesman of the highest rank has used the following words: " I say that is a most dangerous proceeding when you are dealing in the country districts of England with a population new to political duties, and not as yet educated to the same pitch of political culture as happily prevails in our great centres of population. They are easily misled by promises, by the prospect of schemes which can never be fulfilled. Their members, recollect, are not reported to the same extent that the members of the great towns are reported; they go about from one small meeting to another, dropping here a promise and there something not quite a promise, but which is taken as such; and it is all-important to them, as they despair of winning the educated urban electors, to do what they can to convert the uncultured rural electors."

I believe this to be a reasonably close approximation to the mental condition of those men who still "plough the glebe and lop the glades"—the *bonâ fide* agricultural labourers of this country. It is easy to see, however, that here are materials for the revolutionary agitator to work upon; and one of the most important, if not *the* most important, social questions of the present day, is how best to counteract his efforts. For all honest and conscientious endeavours to elevate the condition of the peasantry, without any *arrière-pensée* in the background, we have the most unfeigned respect. But it is perfectly well known that a detachment of Radicals are now busily at work who only make the improvement of the peasantry a stalking-horse for the destruction of the gentry; and it is against these, and *their* dealings with the peasantry, that we have to be on our guard. The country gentlemen are marked men with a certain set of politicians. A triple attack is gradually being developed against their property, their influence, and their amusements. Their estates are threatened by the compulsory appropriation of land for purposes of very doubtful utility. Their influence is threatened by the transfer of their local duties to other hands. And their amusements are threatened by the Cockney clamour which is still kept up against all manner of field-sports. To compel them to retire from the position which they now occupy by robbing it of all which makes it either dignified or pleasant, is the scarcely disguised object of one section of "the labourer's friends."

Should anybody think that the language here used is unjust or exaggerated, he may compare the words of perhaps the ablest of English journals, whose Liberalism is above suspicion. On the 14th of April 1888, the 'Spectator' wrote as follows of the proposed parish council: "If he [the squire] stood for election, he would be catechised, criticised, and ridiculed throughout his own domain; and if he did not stand, he would be left stranded with no means of influence, and no rights except that of obeying orders, which, if the control of pathways is handed over to the parish councils, will often be dictated by pure malice and a desire to humiliate the local king."

The Church, too, is an integral part of the English rural system; and it is only to be expected that the Radical party in the parish or district councils will, sooner or later, claim the right of interference with the parish churches. On all these subjects the labourer will be appealed to by the usual arguments. And the question is how far he has the intellectual stamina to hold out against the fallacies that will be laid before him, when they seem to promise him any immediate material advantage.

So far we have contented ourselves with registering the distinction which must just now be drawn between the higher and lower grades of the English peasantry—between those who are attracted to the towns and those who remain upon the land. But when we have done this, there are still other distinctions to be drawn, and modifications and reservations to be taken into account besides. All the superior class of labourers have not left the land. All the inferior class are not such as I have described. All villages are not alike— the difference between those in which there is a resident proprietor, and those in which there is not, being marked, and apparently indelible. And finally, all the cottage population are not agricultural labourers. Thus we shall see that, with all these limitations, the class to which our less favourable estimate applies is not quite so large as might at first sight have been supposed; though I am afraid, at the same time, that the non-agricultural elements of the English peasantry are not of a nature to do much to neutralise any mischievous ingredients which may have crept into the general mass. The small shopkeeper, the tailor, the shoemaker, and the carpenter, in a country village, are not usually either the best Churchmen or the best Conservatives in the parish: for what reason I cannot imagine, unless it is from some inherent moral antagonism between trade of any kind and agriculture, which to the philosopher is foolishness, but which to the practical observer does often seem to be the only explanation of various rural phenomena.

To set against this, however, we have the better disposition and more conservative sentiments of even the present class of labourers in villages which have been for generations under the immediate influence of a resident landed proprietor, and have had average good fortune in the vicars or rectors of the parish. If the trading element in the country goes to weigh down the scale on one side, the lingering spirit of feudal loyalty will depress it on the other. We may allow these two influences perhaps to cancel each other. But even then we have a floating balance of doubtful if not unfriendly feeling to reckon with, which we cannot contemplate without anxiety.

How the present race of labourers would demean themselves with regard to the various questions above mentioned, tithes, compulsory expropriation, wastes, footpaths, game, &c., if appealed to on such matters by candidates for a parish or district council, would be determined very much by the presence or absence of the conditions to which I have just referred. Where the squire and the parson were resident, and did their duty to the people—as in ninety-nine cases out of every hundred, where they are resident, they do do it—

there it is likely that much of the agitator's eloquence would be exerted in vain. Where this wholesome influence was wanting, it would probably as a rule prevail. The English peasantry, I repeat, have, as a body, no desire to annoy their superiors. But there are two or three questions on which they feel strongly. They are tenacious of what they suppose to be their right to roadside wastes. They are sensitive on the subject of footpaths. And though I am quite certain they do not wish to see game exterminated, they are irritated by the severity with which petty breaches of the gamelaws are occasionally punished. Now in regard to their behaviour on these questions, the character of the men they lived under would just make the entire difference. If they felt that on the whole there was an honest desire, on the part of the gentry and clergy, to consult their comfort and convenience, and to regard trifling offences with lenity, then they would act upon the principle of give and take, and would not insist too obstinately on their own claims, whether real or imaginary. But where this was not felt, or where there was nothing to soften down the friction usually created by bailiffs, agents, middlemen of all kinds, and gamekeepers, then the peasantry would be very likely to show their teeth, and in some cases to regulate their votes by pure malice. Leave him to the promptings of his own unbiassed disposition under what I call the natural and healthy conditions of rural life, and I do not believe the labourer would raise a finger to cut up the estate of any neighbouring proprietor against his will. But even apart from this, I do not think that under the conditions I am supposing he would desire to injure the gentry in order even to benefit himself. The misfortune is, that in so many parts of England these conditions are absent, and the danger is lest the sins of a small class of country gentlemen should be visited on the whole body.

We must remember, too, that in many parts of England the social influence of the gentry has been grievously impaired by the agricultural depression, making absentees of them against their will, and leaving rural society without its natural leaders and directors. It must be allowed that the reconstruction of county government took place at a very unfortunate moment, when the old landed proprietors were in a worse position for contending with Radical hostility than they had ever occupied before. Perhaps with the returning tide of agricultural prosperity the old instincts may revive, and the alarm created by recent legislation be looked back upon as a passing panic. It may be so; and practical Conservatives, to quote the words of Lord Monmouth, in 'Coningsby,' "must say so, and try to believe so."

What has been said of parish councils does not equally apply to district councils, which would be much better fitted for dealing with the ordinary wants of English villages than the more august body which is elected by the whole county. The area covered by the district council would be sufficiently small to admit of its members being acquainted with all the parishes contained in it, while it would be large enough to afford some security for a due admixture of the various elements of rural life in the governing body, and to prevent the narrowest and pettiest local jealousies from obtaining an absolute preponderance. It seems indeed almost inevitable, even if parish councils were instituted, that district councils should be intermixed with them. There are some parishes so thinly populated, that to give them a council would be like restoring members to Old Sarum. Such places *must* be grouped with others, and it would be far simpler to plant district councils at once in areas corresponding as nearly as might be with the poor-law unions.

Since the introduction of county councils the district council has become a necessity. The country gentry and magistrates, to whom our rural administration was formerly intrusted, had the local knowledge required for it. The county council as a body has not. And it is essential, therefore, to establish some smaller authority possessing this essential qualification. Of course the district council will afford a field for the agitator, as well as the parochial, and attempts will be made to use the one for the same purposes as the 'Spectator' tells us we are to anticipate from the other. But it will not be so easy to turn the larger assembly to the same account; and it is to be hoped, after all, that things have not gone so far in England yet as to ensure the triumph of Radicalism in the rural districts. The English peasantry are nowhere alienated like the Irish. They are easily affected by kindness and liberality, and it is only here and there that respect for the ancient proprietors of the soil is absolutely extinguished. There is still time for the country gentlemen to revive the loyalty of the labourers wherever it has decayed, by meeting them halfway in all their new aspirations, and by saying to them in effect, and in language they would glady listen to—" We will be your leaders."

Of all the classes of which civilised society is composed, the agricultural, says Aristotle, is the least given to sedition. And there is an inherent conservatism in the English peasantry which will long struggle against the sweeping changes recommended to them, however apparently favourable to their own interests. There is nothing so conservative as Nature. And the labourer passes his days from the cradle to the grave in communion with her. The woods and brooks and hills, the corn and pasture fields, the unchanging landmarks which greet him every day as he goes forth to and returns from his labours, make a man think less of himself than he does when pent up in cities amid the work of human hands, and the incessant din of social rivalries and controversies. The trees and the fields speak to him in a different voice. They speak to him of that which is tranquil, permanent, and beautiful, rebuking not only "the fierce tumultuous passions," but also all the little petty animosities of this fleeting existence. This is what Virgil was thinking of in those delightful lines—

"Fortunatus et ille, Deos qui novit agrestes,
Panaque Sylvanumque senem, Nymphasque sorores!"

Though unconscious of the source from which it comes, it is hence that the peasant derives much of that composure of manner and that natural dignity which is one of his generic characteristics. There is a natural courtesy and politeness in the country labourers, where they have not been brutalised by long neglect, which it is very pleasant to experience, and which would make it doubly

painful should there ever come to be a class war
between the peasantry and the gentry. I will not
believe for a moment that these manners are assumed by the labourers to serve their own purposes
or disguise their real feelings. Let a stranger
during a country walk ask any labouring man at
work in the fields his way to the next village,
or the name of the owner of the land, or any
other question concerning the neighbourhood, and
observe the manner of his reply. It is quite easy
and natural; at the same time perfectly respectful. He conveys the impression that he likes to
be spoken to, and he is evidently anxious to oblige.
This is not the manner of the townsman, who, I
believe, at heart is equally willing to be of service
to you, but has not the faculty of conveying his
information in the same agreeable and good-hu-
moured manner as the rustic. The latter is never
in a false position; never on the alert to detect
any fancied slight in your mode of addressing him;
never uneasy for fear you should be thinking too
little of him: he knows his own station, and what
is due to himself; and as long as you show that

you know it too, he is perfectly satisfied, and never afraid of being too complaisant. This natural ease is the secret of good-breeding in all classes. It is self-consciousness that makes men awkward; and to this failing the peasant is a total stranger.

He is indebted for its absence partly to the life he leads, and partly to the fact that he has till lately been satisfied with his lot, and animated by no social jealousies or ambitions. The mere fact that he is not struggling for admission into any higher sphere of society than his own, but is satisfied to be what he is, and to know that nothing more is expected of him than what is proper to that station, tends to put a man at his ease; and herein the peasant will contrast very favourably with the artisan.

This last remark, however, applies, it must be owned, rather to the generation that is going off the stage than to the one that is coming on. And what a pleasant generation it was! I have lived with them, played with them, ate and drank with them, gone bird-nesting with them, shot and fished with them, and talked with them by the hour while they were threshing in the old barn with the good old flail—whose sound perhaps I shall never hear again—or cutting and "layering" the stiff whitethorn hedges with their short billhooks and huge leather gantlets, standing up to their ankles in the water at the bottom of the ditch from eight o'clock in the morning to four o'clock in the afternoon. Such men were ignorant of many things which village children of ten years old understand now. But they had a natural shrewdness and sense of humour which always made their conversation interesting, and were as free from any taint of what is commonly called vulgarity as the finest lady in the land. They were indeed Nature's gentlemen. They never tried to talk fine. They used their own rustic language without shame, and thinking no evil; and I even recollect a most worthy old villager and excellent Churchman who habitually addressed the vicar's daughter, a lady of seven or eight and twenty, as "my wench," to the intense amusement and delight of the lady herself, so naturally and politely was it said, so evidently meant as a mark of affection and regard from one who had known her from the cradle. When the young peasantry become old, they won't be able to do this, I am afraid.

The remarks of their seniors in the region of religion and morality were usually the most racy and characteristic. I remember a woman in our parish, a tall masculine female, and something of a termagant, though not ill disposed upon the whole, and always respectful to her betters, from whom the clergyman's daughter, after giving her some spiritual admonitions, received the following answer: "Well, miss, I like to hear you talk in that way, and I daresay it's very good and very true; but we poor folks, we've got to scrat a living together—*we must chance it.*"

On another occasion a serious pedlar made his appearance in the village, declaring to every cottage matron who opened her door to him that times were very bad, and that he didn't know what he should do "if he hadn't a sure hope through grace." "For my part," said a labourer's wife, explaining the pedlar's source of confidence, "I leave bragging to others."

Well, all these old people will soon be laid in their narrow cells, and with them much sterling honesty, shrewd sense, fidelity and simplicity. New questions which they never understood will be agitated over their graves, and new conditions of rural life may gradually emerge from the hurly-burly which the most inveterate idolater of the past will, if he lives to witness them, acknowledge to be improvements. But while it is yet doubtful whether this result will follow, we cannot help casting a longing lingering look at the ancient race, with their antique virtues and simple kindly manners, and devoutly hoping that the greater enlightenment of the new generation may compensate for their absence.

In bringing this series of sketches to a close while we are still in the middle of the great scheme for the reconstruction of county administration, I feel that I am taking an appropriate farewell of that old *régime* to which they have been principally dedicated. It may be that under the new one the distribution of power will not be materially altered, and that for many years to come the rural system of England may present an unchanged exterior. It may be so, though I am not one of those who look forward to this result with much confidence. But if the form remains, the spirit will have flown — the moral atmosphere will be different. We have been looking back upon a past which has no doubt been a period of transition, much that still survived at the commencement of it having gradually passed away before either the county franchise or the county council came in to complete the transformation. But it is equally true that men between fifty and sixty can recall a time when the setting sun of patriarchal feudalism had not yet sunk below the horizon, and still shed a lingering glow upon the face of rural England. Our eyes have been watching its expiring beams, as they slowly faded away from one picturesque object after another, and we have only ventured to steal a few furtive glances at the evening clouds to ask what they might tell us of the morning. We have stood with our backs to the future, drinking

in the sweetness of the olden time, rendered all
the sweeter by the thought that it was slipping
from our grasp, indulging our sympathies to the
utmost, and feeling in the words of the old song
that to-morrow we'd get sober—" Cras ingens itera-
bimus æquor." The most sanguine of us can hardly
expect that such remnants of saturnian times as
may still survive at this moment will outlive the
new influences now brought to bear upon them,
or that the little village hierarchy can be ever
again what it once was. The chairman of the
county council may be a country gentleman,
with country gentlemen on his right and on
his left. The farmers may recover their spirits,
regain their equanimity, and exhibit their former
common-sense; the labourers may find out that the
city, after all, is a bad exchange for the country,
and come back again to the fields and villages.
All this may happen, and yet the whole result
will be different, and the only question is whether
more than all this will not happen. The past
may glide away from us without any violent dis-
ruption of the old ties which still remain unbroken,

or amidst a convulsive conflict leaving a legacy of feuds behind it. The show may remain when the substance has departed, or both show and substance may collapse together. But be this as it may, the 1st of January 1889 will hereafter be looked back upon as an epoch in our rural history and our national life, when we stood at the parting of the ways and elected to try an experiment which, whether it strengthen or weaken the foundations of a system which has lasted for eight hundred years, inaugurates a social revolution not inferior in magnitude to any which have occurred in England during the last two centuries.

THE EIGHTEENTH CENTURY.

CARRYING back our retrospect of "the ancient *régime*" into the eighteenth century, we see that the old is not divided from the new by any fixed line of demarcation separating the two centuries from each other. The boundary is not chronological, nor yet perfectly straight. At several points the old century overlaps the new one. The change begins earlier in one place and later in another: and here and there old habits and manners run down into the modern age, unthawed by the sun of progress which has melted everything else around them. But they have lost one main characteristic of the earlier period. As we contemplate the eighteenth century, one of the first things to strike us is the air of repose which breathes over it. It reminds one of the land of the lotus-eaters, "in which it seemed always afternoon." One generation succeeded to another, but life continued just the same. The old man saw in his age the things which he had seen in his youth. That longing for confirmed tranquillity which Wordsworth speaks of as one of the strongest instincts of our nature, might then be satisfied. At the present day we never know how soon any of our old landmarks, be they customs, institutions, beliefs, or even the mere features of nature, may be ruthlessly demolished. We scarcely dare allow our affections to go out from us to twine themselves round any external object, for fear it should be suddenly torn up. To be afraid to love anything, for fear we should be obliged to mourn for it, is one form of human unhappiness for which heavy compensation of some kind is due to us at the hands of progress. The eighteenth century had little progress; but then it had little worry, and no doubt. The most ardent Ritualist nowadays, says Mr Froude, feels that the ground is hollow under him. The most sanguine Conservative knows that institutions are everywhere on their trial, that authority is everywhere disputed, that subordination is everywhere derided. But to the men of the eighteenth century none of these disquieting elements presented themselves. Everything around them breathed of permanence, stability, and security; institutions were regarded as facts about which it was ridiculous to argue. It was not supposed possible that we could do without the Church and the Monarchy. There was a reality and solidity about men's convictions in those days which must have been a great source of moral and intellectual comfort. Happy they who lived in the prescientific age! Happy Old Leisure, sauntering by his garden wall, and picking the leaves off the apricots! Happy old vicar, smoking his pipe in peace, unvexed of Darwins and Colensos, scratching the head of his faithful old brown setter, with his old single-barrelled flint-and-steel in the corner by his side!

I am inclined to believe that with some qualities, which the general consent of mankind has till quite recent times esteemed highly beneficial to society, the eighteenth century was more largely endowed than its successor. I mean respect for law and constituted authority as such, and that kind of rational self-knowledge which recognises the facts of human nature, and not only sees nothing degrading in subordination, but accepts it as the one essential principle of all permanent political communities. I hope I shall not be so far misunderstood as to be supposed to deny that there is any other kind of earnestness. There is the earnestness of curiosity and inquiry; the earnestness which seeks the law within the law. But there is also the earnestness which comes of a simple desire to perform our allotted duties under the system of things which we find to be in existence, and asks for no higher satisfaction than the consciousness of having been successful. I cannot help thinking that of this kind of earnestness there was rather more in the past century than there is in the present. The motto of Englishmen then was *Spartam nactus es*: and it was, I think, the mixture of this simple sense of duty with the

somewhat tougher moral fibre of the period which
produced such men as Clive and Hastings and many
of our great Indian and colonial administrators,
with whom their duty to their country was an all-
sufficient motive of action and ample warrant for
the means they might adopt in the discharge of it.

When it is said that the eighteenth century was
not an age of faith, the statement can only be
received with considerable reservation, and in reference to a sphere of thought far removed above the
level even of the middle classes. "The sober piety"
of our ancestors has come in for its full share of
laughter. Yet it is doubtful if more solid fruits
were not borne by this uninteresting tree than are
produced either by the fervour of ritualism or the
inspiration of "Humanity." Whether it is a fact or
not that English work, for instance, has fallen off
since the eighteenth century in thoroughness and
honesty, I do not undertake to say; but the affirmative has been widely maintained, without, as far as
I know, provoking any serious contradiction, and
has been acknowledged with regret by some of
the warmest friends and admirers of the working

classes. The evil, however, if it really exist, is not confined to them. Small traders of every description are charged with selling and constructing articles which are not what they represent them to be; and that old English pride in a good piece of honest work which was once so general is said to be growing rarer and rarer. If so, I cannot imagine anything better calculated to make us doubtful of the superior religious earnestness of the present day.

The coarseness of private manners was only one form of the general licence which was the inevitable product of the Revolution. It was not till late in the eighteenth century that society began to recover from the moral shock occasioned by the rupture of old ties, the rejection of old sanctions, and the extinction of an old faith which followed that event. The ideal, romantic, or imaginative element—call it what you will—had been crushed out of Church and State with the expulsion of the Stuarts and the remodelling of our religious institutions on a rational basis. The inevitable result was an influx among the upper classes of both political and religious indifference, which, where it did not end in absolute scepticism, was wholly ineffectual against the temptations of the world and the flesh. The influence, in a word, of the English Revolution upon English morals was the influence of all revolutions upon all morals in all ages of the world. Political infidelity is their first fruit, and social licence their second. But a change began to show itself after the middle of the century. We hear no more of such doings as went on with Queen Caroline's maids of honour; of such letters as may be found in the correspondence of Lady Suffolk. Mr Lecky has noticed, in a very interesting passage, the concurrent influence of Wesley and Lord Chatham in this purification of the atmosphere. To these names may be added those of Johnson and Cowper. Chatham in politics, Wesley in religion, and Johnson and Cowper in literature, were working for the same end. Chatham infused a wholly new tone into the language of public men. Wesley recalled society to some small consideration for its eternal welfare; and Johnson showed how a man of infinite humour, robust common-sense, and of a strong animal nature, could place them all at the service of religion and worship.

We see the same mixture of good and evil, the same moral indifference, and the same practical excellence in the sphere of politics. The old Cavalier, who represented feudal chivalry, the old Whig, who represented classical freedom, were alike extinct. In the place of the latter we had the practical common-sense politician who wasn't "squeamish," who saw his way to conducting the business of the country without ideas, and to making a good thing out of it for himself; who undertook, so to speak, the beef-and-pudding department of government, and gave a kind of guarantee that nobody should be worried about anything so as to injure his digestion, if he would only abstain from worrying others. "Live and let live," was his motto. And of living he was prepared to set a first-rate example. In place of the former we had the spasmodic patriot, who tried hard, and in one particular successfully, to make national grievances stand him instead of loyalty, but who felt himself commonly in a false position, and always had to cover the weakness of his logic under sounding rhetorical generalities. Both alike, however, had banished idealism from politics, as it had been banished from philosophy and theology. The want of it made the Whigs mercenary utilitarians, and the Tories visionary declaimers.

But whatever the methods or the vices of the governing class, the country had to be governed. And the business of doing it infused a solid, practical, sagacious element into the English upper class, in which the Continental nobility seemed deficient. And we ought to be thoroughly thankful, whatever be the origin we attribute to the English Revolution, that when they had got what they wanted, our nobility proved equal to the occasion. For though their cupidity and selfishness may at one time have been dangerous to the monarchy, the existence of their order in full vigour and popularity was essential to the constitution. A few words will explain our meaning more fully.

"Despotisms," says Dr Newman, "require great men, constitutions jog on without them." The remark was perfectly just, though it was not original; nor does it express the whole truth upon the subject. If constitutions do not want great men, great men, it may be added, do not always suit constitutions. The essence of a constitution is that no very great degree of power shall be lodged in a single individual. And the highest functions, as a rule, which a statesman can discharge in it, are administrative rather than creative. Of course there will be exceptional periods, when the Minister of a constitutional State is, by tacit consent, invested with much larger powers—when he can originate and really govern. This was the case with Mr Pitt; the union of Great Britain and Ireland, for instance, having been entirely his own idea, and carried by his own will. But if we look back upon our parliamentary history, we shall see that the most successful Ministers have been men of very different calibre,—Walpole, Pelham, Liverpool, Palmerston, unlike as they were in other things, all resembled each other in this, that their characteristics were strong common-sense, great capacity for business, and an easy temper.

They had not the creative or inventive faculty which, under this sober and mechanical form of government, is frequently a burden to its possessor. They were content to keep things as they found them, and were satisfied with the dignity of authority. The first Napoleon said of the Duke of Wellington after the battle of Waterloo: "He can never lie quiet—he will change the dynasty." The Duke did not happen to belong to that class of great men. But it shows what Napoleon expected from a man of his exceptional genius. Bolingbroke did belong to that class, and would never have found any scope for his powers under a constitutional government in quiet and ordinary times.

It is the same with what are called men of the people, or men who without influence, without connections, and without money, force themselves to the summit of affairs. They will be imaginative, restless, and daringly ambitious. The very struggle has made them combative and sanguine. Men of this kind are not the men to "jog on." Such characters make great kings and conquerors, and are fitted for the dictatorship of a great democracy.

In constitutional States they are likely to be either useless or dangerous. The English aristocracy produces just the class of men who are wanted for the work in question. It is not ambition in the ordinary sense of the word that leads them into politics. A political life comes to them just as naturally as commerce to the son of a merchant. They think no more of filling a public department than of taking the chair at quarter-sessions. They are neither dazzled by the prospect of power, nor intoxicated by the possession of it. And the consequence is, that a man in that rank of life is not obliged to be gifted with extraordinary genius in order to attain political power, nor, if gifted with extraordinary genius, is it certain that political power will attract him. From the aristocracy we get, as a rule, the able, sagacious, business-like men whom the country wants, but who would not have forced their way upwards from a lower station; not the turbulent restless spirits who, if they take to politics at all, destroy institutions and change dynasties. We want such men sometimes; but in democracies they come too often, and hence their proverbial instability. There are drawbacks, of course, to an aristocratic system. We cannot expect such men to be abstract philosophers, to know by heart Aristotle's 'Politics' or Mill's 'Political Economy.' But there is no dearth of such knowledge at the present day among those who can influence politics through the periodical press; and if the truth must be told, we are in danger rather of having too much of it than of having too little.

I often think of the eighteenth century as a broad rich plain lying between two volcanic ranges; a happy valley, rich in corn and wine and oil, to say nothing of ale and punch, and, if defective in those virtues which thrive best in a stonier soil, not without a goodness of its own which demands our genuine respect, and certainly pregnant with results to which we owe a deep debt of gratitude. It was not a century overburdened with delicacy or scrupulousness of any kind, but bluff, hale, and hearty; a century of great moral and mental tranquillity, of some coarseness and animalism, and of unruffled religious belief among the great masses of the people; a century in which abuses were allowed to spread in prodigal luxuriance over all our most venerable institutions, but in which the landmarks were not removed, nor habits rudely disturbed; a century of strong men and strong deeds, in which England rose to a predominant place among the nations of the world, and fitted herself to perform the great part which was in store for her as the saviour of the liberties of Europe.

Many of its characteristics lingered late into the succeeding age. Rural life during the first quarter of the nineteenth century must in many respects have been much the same as in the last quarter of the eighteenth. To a much later period than this individuals still survived who had far more in common with the Georgian than the Victorian era; while among the peasantry, at all events, habits and customs and character had been transmitted unchanged from the rude forefathers of the hamlet, whose epitaph is written by Gray. Now, however, I think we are really getting on the *extrema vestigia* of the ancient *régime*. Now at length, for the first time, the destruction of our ancient rural system is openly avowed as their object by a powerful political party in this country. Through all the changes we have experienced since 1832, reformers have never, till within the last few years, proclaimed any intention of subverting it. Whatever they might think or say to each other in private, no one of them ever publicly stated that it was his object to crush the Church and the landed gentry. This dead set at "the squire and the parson," is an affair of yesterday. It may be that it was certain to come. But changes are not necessarily beneficial because they are inevitable, or what a paradise this world would be. At all events, it will scarcely be denied that our old rural system had much in it to touch the imagination, and appealed to a class of sentiments not wholly bad. I am therefore not without a hope that these pages may at least be found interesting, even to many who differ from myself; and that to recall to men's minds the class of virtues, both public and private, which are proper to an age of territorial aristocracy, when it is allowed a fair field for its energies, showing that in the progress to democracy the gain is not all on one side, may not at the present moment be labour altogether thrown away.

THE END.

PRINTED BY WILLIAM BLACKWOOD AND SONS.

www.ingramcontent.com/pod-product-compliance
Lightning Source LLC
Chambersburg PA
CBHW031747230426
43669CB00007B/521